cind.-n-
True
Love

Don+ Broke
My hart

Case I Love
you.So
Don+ Diet

My
that
cind
R

Kim.F -n- Pat.p
True
Love

Don't O

Its My Hart
Pat and Cind
Kim.F

L'gvt

Better Homes and Gardens®
Recipes for Entertaining

Peach Crepes is a spectacular dessert that's sure to impress guests. Prepare the mixture in a chafing dish, then spoon servings onto dessert plates before watchful eyes.

On the cover: This appetizer buffet for 20 features *Tomato Tidbits, Shrimp Dip, Sweet-Sour Franks,* and *Smoky Cheese Ball,* plus the delicious beverage, *Lemon-Apple Sparkle.*

BETTER HOMES AND GARDENS BOOKS

Editorial Director: Don Dooley
Managing Editor: Malcolm E. Robinson   Art Director: John Berg
Food Editor: Nancy Morton
Senior Food Editor: Joyce Trollope
Associate Editors: Sharyl Heiken, Rosalie Riglin
Assistant Editors: Sandra Mapes, Elizabeth Strait
Copy Editor: Lawrence Clayton
Designer: Harijs Priekulis

CONTENTS

Our seal assures you that every recipe in *Recipes For Entertaining*
is endorsed by the Better Homes and Gardens Test Kitchen. Each
recipe is tested for family appeal, practicality, and deliciousness.

LET'S HAVE A PARTY

"Let's have a party!" is an invitation to have fun with friends or new acquaintances. Both you and your guests will enjoy yourselves if you take the time to plan and execute the party well. Sound hard? It's not. Not if you take advantage of the many recipes, menus, and the sound advice given in *Recipes for Entertaining*.

If you want to entertain friends, but can't think of a reason for doing so, remember: Any reason is a good one. If there are no special occasions listed on your calendar, make up something. Celebrate the first day of Spring, a moon landing, your child's first step, a pay raise, anything.

Once you've settled this, pull *Recipes for Entertaining* down off the shelf and start browsing through it. One of the first things you'll notice about the book is that it is divided in such a way that regardless of the size of your gathering—that's within reason, of course—there are menus and recipes to accommodate your plans. Quite an advantage over most cook books.

You'll also notice that a vast number of serving occasions are covered in the book—breakfast, brunch, luncheon, fondue party, semiformal dinner, holiday family dinner, buffet dinner, teen party, make-a-pizza party, potluck supper, after-the-game supper, picnic, appetizer buffet, shower, and many others. This large selection is helpful to you in two ways: It makes the book versatile; and it gives you a good idea of the many entertaining opportunities at your fingertips.

Recipes for Entertaining will answer many questions for you, too. It will tell you how to plan a party from beginning to end, how to set the table properly, and what table appointments to use. There are also pointers on etiquette. In addition, it will tell you how to be an organized, well-prepared host or hostess.

In short, *Recipes for Entertaining* tells you everything you have to know about entertaining to have a successful gathering. That's a promise.

Parties for 4 to 8 people

If the invitation list for your next party includes only a few guests, remember that a small gathering has several advantages. For one thing, serving dinner to a small group permits you to splurge a bit by preparing lobster, steak, or other individual foods without ruining your food budget.

Another advantage is that you will probably have enough seating space, china, glassware, and flatware for a sit-down dinner. A meal of this kind allows you to display your cooking prowess by preparing part of the meal at the table in a chafing dish, an electric skillet, or a wok.

So, *stop* worrying about what to serve, *look* at the recipes in this section, and *heed* the information given. Sound easy? It is! Happy party-giving.

Cook *Chicken-Steak Almond* at the table in a wok or an electric skillet for an intimate dinner for four. Accompany with crispy chow mein noodles, steamed rice, *Cucumber-Radish Plate*, and warm sake.

RECIPES

(For appetizer and snack recipes see pages 98 to 103. Recipes especially suited for small groups include Yogurt-Cuke Dip, Smoked Oyster Dip, Notches, and Smoked Salmon Rolls.)

Christmas Onion Soup

    1½ large onions
    2 tablespoons butter or margarine
    1 tablespoon all-purpose flour
    1 quart milk
    2 beaten egg yolks
      Parmesan cheese
      French bread slices

Thinly slice onions and separate into rings (3 cups); cook in butter till tender but not brown, about 10 minutes. Sprinkle with flour; cook and stir over low heat till blended. Add milk; cover and simmer 20 minutes. Add 1 teaspoon salt and dash pepper. Stir small amount hot mixture into yolks. Return to hot mixture, stirring till blended. Season to taste. Sprinkle each serving with cheese; serve hot with bread. Makes 8 first-course servings.

Oysters en Brochette

    1 pint shucked oysters (24)
    12 slices partially cooked bacon
    1 6-ounce can whole mushrooms, drained (about 1 cup)
    1 large green pepper, cut in squares
    ¼ cup butter or margarine, melted
    1 tablespoon lemon juice
      Dash garlic powder

Drain oysters; halve bacon. Wrap *each* oyster with bacon. Thread on 6 short skewers, alternating with mushrooms and green pepper. Place in shallow baking pan. Combine remaining ingredients, ¼ teaspoon salt, and dash pepper; brush over oysters and vegetables. Bake at 450° for 10 minutes; brush with butter mixture. Makes 6 first-course servings.

Fruit Cup Starter

Chill and drain one 16-ounce can orange and grapefruit sections and one 8-ounce can seedless grapes. Spoon fruit into 4 sherbet dishes. Blend together ½ cup pineapple yogurt and 1 tablespoon sugar. Drizzle yogurt over fruit. Makes 4 first-course servings.

Clam-Baked Lobster

    2 large or 4 small live lobsters
    2 beaten eggs
    1 10½-ounce can condensed cream of celery soup
    2 tablespoons snipped parsley
    ½ teaspoon onion salt
    2 7½-ounce cans minced clams
    4 cups plain croutons
    ¼ cup butter or margarine, melted

Select active lobsters; plunge headfirst into enough boiling, salted water to cover. Cook 2 minutes. Place lobsters, on their backs, on cutting board. With sharp knife split soft undershell lengthwise from head to tail (remove head, if desired). Using shears, snip out undershell membrane on tail section. Discard all organs in body section except liver and red coral roe. Remove black vein that runs down tail. Crack claws. Place, cut side up, in shallow baking pan. Combine next 4 ingredients and dash pepper. (Add liver and roe, if desired.) Drain clams, reserving ¼ cup liquid. Stir clams and reserved liquid into soup mixture. Add croutons; toss to coat. Spoon into lobsters. Bake at 350° for 30 to 35 minutes. Drizzle with butter during baking. Serves 4.

Seafood fare

Entice your guests with one of these special → dishes: *Clam-Baked Lobster, Oysters en Brochette,* or *Land and Sea Salad* (see page 10).

Land and Sea Salad

      4 cups torn mixed salad greens
      1½ pounds frozen king crab legs,
            thawed and shelled, *or* 1 6-ounce
            package frozen crab meat, thawed,
            or 1 7½-ounce can crab meat,
            drained and cartilage removed
      1 pound shrimp, cooked, peeled, and
            deveined
      1 cup cherry tomatoes, halved
      2 tablespoons sliced green onion
      1 large avocado
      Curry Dressing

In salad bowl top greens with crab meat, shrimp, cherry tomato halves, and green onion; chill. Just before serving, peel and slice avocado; add to salad. Toss with chilled Curry Dressing. Makes 6 servings.

Curry Dressing: Stir together 1 cup mayonnaise or salad dressing; ¼ cup milk; 1 clove garlic, minced; 2 teaspoons curry powder; ¼ teaspoon Worcestershire sauce; and 6 to 8 drops bottled hot pepper sauce. Chill.

Deviled Lamb Chops

      2 tablespoons all-purpose flour
      ½ teaspoon garlic salt
      ½ teaspoon dried thyme, crushed
      4 lamb shoulder chops, ½ inch thick
      2 tablespoons salad oil
      Prepared mustard
      ½ cup chicken broth
      1 medium onion, sliced
      4 green pepper rings
      4 thin slices lemon
      ¼ teaspoon salt
      1 tablespoon all-purpose flour

Combine first 3 ingredients; use to coat chops. In skillet brown the chops in hot oil. Spread each chop with mustard; add broth and onion. Cover; simmer 25 minutes. Add green pepper, lemon, and salt. Cover; cook till meat is tender, about 10 minutes more. Remove chops, onion, lemon, and pepper to warm platter. Combine ¼ cup water and 1 tablespoon flour; stir into pan drippings. Cook and stir till thickened; pour over chops. Makes 4 servings.

Artichokes à la Ham Curry

      4 artichokes
      2 cups ground fully cooked ham
      ½ cup chopped onion
      2 tablespoons salad oil
      ¼ cup fine dry bread crumbs
      2 beaten eggs
      ¼ cup snipped parsley
      Curry Sauce

Wash artichokes; cut one inch from entire top. Cut stem close to base. Pull off dry, loose leaves. Simmer artichokes, covered, in boiling, salted water till stalk can be easily pierced and a leaf pulled out readily, 25 to 30 minutes. Drain upside down. Snip off sharp leaf tips. Remove center leaves and chokes.

In skillet cook ham and onion in hot oil till onion is tender. Add crumbs, eggs, parsley, and ¼ teaspoon pepper; mix well. Spread artichoke leaves apart slightly; fill center of each artichoke with ham mixture. Place in a 9x9x2-inch baking pan. Pour hot water around artichokes to a depth of 1 inch. Bake, uncovered, at 375° about 30 minutes. Serve with Curry Sauce. Makes 4 servings.

Curry Sauce: In small saucepan combine 1 cup dairy sour cream, ⅓ cup milk, 1 teaspoon curry powder, and ¼ teaspoon salt. Heat, stirring occasionally. Do not boil.

Pork Loin with Orange Stuffing

      1 5-pound pork loin
      ¼ cup chopped onion
      2 tablespoons butter or margarine
      2 tablespoons frozen orange juice
            concentrate, thawed
      1 cup herb-seasoned stuffing mix
      ¼ teaspoon ground sage

Have meatman loosen backbone of pork loin and cut pockets between chops. Cook onion in butter till tender. Add ¼ cup water and juice concentrate; mix well. Toss with stuffing mix and sage. Spoon 2 tablespoons stuffing between each chop. Place on rack in shallow roasting pan. Roast at 325° till meat thermometer registers 170°, about 2½ to 3 hours. Remove backbone before serving. Serves 8.

Ham-Rice Bake

Double recipe and bake in 13½x8¾x1¾-inch baking dish about 30 minutes for 12 servings—

    3 cups cubed fully cooked ham
    ⅔ cup long grain rice, cooked
    1 tablespoon snipped parsley
    ⅓ cup chopped onion
    4 tablespoons butter
    3 tablespoons all-purpose flour
    2 cups milk
    3 beaten eggs
    1 tablespoon prepared
        mustard
    ¾ cup soft bread crumbs

Combine ham, hot rice, and parsley. Cook onion in *3 tablespoons butter;* blend in flour, ½ teaspoon salt, and ⅛ teaspoon pepper. Add milk all at once. Cook and stir till thickened and bubbly. Stir *half* the hot mixture into eggs; return to saucepan and cook 1 minute more. Blend in mustard. Stir sauce into ham mixture. Pour into a 10x6x1¾-inch baking dish. Melt remaining butter; stir in crumbs. Sprinkle atop casserole. Bake at 350° for 25 to 30 minutes. Let stand 5 minutes. Serves 6.

Corn-Stuffed Pork Chops

    8 pork loin chops, ¼ inch thick
    1 cup chopped celery
    ½ cup chopped onion
    ¼ cup butter or margarine
    4 cups soft bread crumbs
    1 8¾-ounce can whole kernel
        corn, drained
    ½ teaspoon rubbed sage
        Paprika

Season the chops with salt and pepper. Cook celery and onion in butter till tender but not brown. Combine cooked vegetables, crumbs, corn, ½ teaspoon salt, sage, and dash pepper. Place *half* the chops on rack in shallow roasting pan. Spoon about ⅔ cup stuffing onto each; top with remaining chops. Cover pan with foil; bake at 325° for 45 minutes. Remove foil and bake till meat is tender, about 30 minutes more. Sprinkle with paprika. Makes 4 servings.

Cranberry Pork Chops

    8 pork rib chops, ¾ inch thick
    2 tablespoons shortening
    1 8-ounce can whole cranberry sauce
    ¼ cup bottled barbecue sauce
    4 teaspoons cornstarch
        Hot cooked rice

In a skillet brown the chops in hot shortening. Season with salt and pepper. Drain off excess fat. Combine cranberry sauce, barbecue sauce, and ¼ cup water; pour over chops. Cover and simmer till chops are tender, 45 to 55 minutes. Remove the chops to warm platter; keep hot. Combine cornstarch and 2 tablespoons cold water. Stir into sauce in skillet. Cook and stir till thickened and bubbly. Spoon some sauce over chops; pass additional sauce. Serve with hot cooked rice. Makes 8 servings.

Sausage-Filled Crepes

Crepes can be made ahead and refrigerated—

    3 beaten eggs
    1 cup milk
    1 tablespoon salad oil
    1 cup sifted all-purpose flour
        Sausage Filling
    ¼ cup butter or margarine, softened
    ¼ cup dairy sour cream

Combine first 3 ingredients. Add flour and ½ teaspoon salt; beat till smooth. Pour 2 tablespoons batter into greased 6-inch skillet; tilt to cover bottom. Cook till browned; invert on paper toweling. Repeat to make 16 crepes.

Place 2 tablespoons Sausage Filling down center of each crepe; roll. Arrange in 11¾x 7½x1¾-inch baking dish. Combine butter and sour cream; spread on crepes. Bake, covered, at 375° for 20 minutes. Makes 6 to 8 servings.

Sausage Filling: In a skillet cook 1 pound bulk pork sausage and ¼ cup chopped onion till browned; drain. Stir in 2 ounces process American cheese, shredded (½ cup); one 3-ounce package cream cheese, softened; ¼ teaspoon celery salt; and ¼ teaspoon dried marjoram, crushed. Remove from heat; stir in ¾ cup dairy sour cream and 1 tablespoon milk.

Beef Fondue

Let guests cook their own meat at the table —

> Salad oil
> 1 teaspoon salt
> 1½ pounds trimmed beef tenderloin,
>   cut in ¾-inch cubes
> Wine Sauce
> Mushroom Sauce

Pour salad oil into metal fondue cooker to no more than ½ capacity or to a depth of 2 inches. Heat over range to 425°. Add salt. Transfer cooker to fondue burner. Have beef at room temperature. Spear meat cube with fondue fork; fry in hot oil to desired doneness. Transfer hot meat to dinner fork; dip in Wine Sauce or Mushroom Sauce. Makes 4 servings.

Fondue Sauces

Wine Sauce: In saucepan stir ¾ cup sauterne into ¼ cup catsup. Bring to boil. Simmer, uncovered, 5 minutes. Blend 2 tablespoons cold water and 4 teaspoons cornstarch; stir into wine mixture. Cook and stir till thickened and bubbly. Add 1 tablespoon butter; cook 1 minute more. Serve hot. Makes ¾ cup.

Mushroom Sauce: Drain one 3-ounce can chopped mushrooms; chop mushrooms more finely. Dissolve 1 beef bouillon cube in ⅔ cup boiling water. In saucepan melt 2 tablespoons butter. Blend in 2 tablespoons all-purpose flour. Add bouillon all at once; mix well. Cook and stir till thickened and bubbly. Stir in ½ cup dairy sour cream, the mushrooms, and 2 teaspoons Worcestershire sauce; heat through. Serve hot. Makes 1⅓ cups.

Arrange mozzarella cheese triangles atop *Sicilian Meat Roll* (made of flavorful ground beef rolled around ham and more cheese). Notice the pinwheel appearance when it is sliced.

Sicilian Meat Roll

A flavorful dish of ground beef, ham, and cheese—

> 2 beaten eggs
> ¾ cup soft bread crumbs (1 slice)
> ½ cup tomato juice
> 2 tablespoons snipped parsley
> ½ teaspoon dried oregano, crushed
> ¼ teaspoon *each* salt and pepper
> 1 clove garlic, minced
> 2 pounds lean ground beef
> 8 thin slices boiled ham
> 6 ounces mozzarella cheese,
>   shredded (1½ cups)
> 3 slices mozzarella cheese, halved
>   diagonally

Combine eggs, crumbs, juice, parsley, oregano, salt, pepper, and garlic. Add beef; mix well. On waxed paper or foil, pat meat to a 12x10-inch rectangle. Arrange ham atop meat, leaving a small margin around edges. Sprinkle shredded cheese over ham. Starting from short end, carefully roll up meat, using paper to lift; seal edges and ends. Place roll, seam side down, in 13x9x2-inch baking pan. Bake at 350° till done, 1¼ hours. (Center of roll will be pink due to ham.) Place cheese wedges over top of roll; return to oven till cheese melts, about 5 minutes. Makes 8 servings.

When making *Sicilian Meat Roll,* pat the meat mixture into a rectangle on waxed paper, then use the paper to aid in rolling meat.

Veal Steak Alaska

> 1 pound veal round steak
> 1 envelope mushroom gravy mix
> 1 3-ounce can sliced mushrooms,
>   drained
> 1 beaten egg
> ½ cup fine dry bread crumbs
> ¼ cup butter or margarine
> 1 7½-ounce can crab meat, drained,
>   flaked, and cartilage removed
> 4 slices process Swiss cheese,
>   halved (4 ounces)

Cut steak into serving-sized pieces; pound to ¼-inch thickness. Prepare gravy mix according to package directions; add mushrooms and keep warm. Dip steaks in egg, then in bread crumbs. In skillet brown steaks in butter; remove from heat. Pile ¼ of the crab meat atop each steak; top with cheese. Return to heat; cook, covered, over medium heat till hot and cheese is melted. Pour gravy into platter; place steaks atop. Makes 4 servings.

Saucy Steak Rolls

> 1½ pounds beef round steak, ¼ inch
>   thick
> ¼ cup finely chopped onion
> 2 tablespoons snipped parsley
> ½ teaspoon dried basil, crushed
> 2 tablespoons all-purpose flour
> 2 tablespoons shortening
> 1 10½-ounce can condensed cream
>   of mushroom soup
> ¼ cup catsup
> 1 teaspoon Worcestershire sauce

Pound meat till very thin; cut into 8 rectangular pieces. Sprinkle lightly with salt and pepper. Divide onion, parsley, and basil between the meat pieces. Roll up jelly-roll fashion, tucking edges in around stuffing. Tie or skewer securely. Coat the meat with flour. In 10-inch skillet brown the meat slowly in hot shortening. Combine soup, catsup, and Worcestershire. Pour over meat. Cover and simmer till meat is tender, about 1¼ hours. Remove cord or skewers before serving. Pass sauce with steak rolls. Makes 4 servings.

Poached Eggs à la King

A perfect dish for a brunch or a luncheon—

½ cup chopped onion
2 tablespoons butter or margarine
1 10½-ounce can condensed cream of
    chicken soup
½ cup milk
6 eggs
3 English muffins, split,
    toasted, and buttered
Snipped parsley

Cook onion in butter till tender. Stir in soup and dash pepper. Blend in milk. Bring to boiling; reduce heat and slip eggs into sauce. Simmer, covered, till eggs are set, 15 minutes. Place *each* egg on muffin half; top with sauce. Sprinkle with parsley. Serves 6.

Chicken and Spaghetti

4 small chicken breasts, split
2 tablespoons shortening
1 1½-ounce envelope spaghetti
    sauce mix
1 8-ounce can tomato sauce
1 3-ounce can sliced mushrooms,
    drained
¼ cup dry red wine
2 tablespoons grated Parmesan cheese
6 ounces spaghetti, cooked and
    drained

Brown the chicken in shortening. Season with salt. Spoon off fat. Combine next 5 ingredients and 1 cup water. Pour over chicken. Cover; simmer 30 minutes. Uncover; simmer till tender, 15 minutes. Serve chicken and sauce over spaghetti. Pass Parmesan, if desired. Serves 4.

Liberally spoon the creamy mushroom sauce over each serving of *Chicken Vol-au-Vent*. The sauce complements the delightful flavor of boned chicken thighs and sausages.

Chicken Vol-au-Vent

   6 chicken thighs (about 1½ pounds)
   2 tablespoons butter or margarine
   1 chicken bouillon cube
   3 tablespoons all-purpose flour
   ¼ teaspoon paprika
   1 cup light cream
   1 6-ounce can sliced mushrooms,
      drained
   ¼ cup dry white wine
   6 brown-and-serve sausages
   1 10-ounce package frozen patty
      shells, thawed (6 shells)

Brown the chicken in butter. Dissolve bouillon in ½ cup hot water; add to chicken. Cover and simmer till tender, 20 to 30 minutes. Remove chicken from broth; cool and remove bones carefully. Measure broth; add water to equal 1 cup liquid. Return to skillet. Combine flour, paprika, ¼ teaspoon salt, and dash pepper; stir in cream. Add to broth; cook and stir till thickened and bubbly. Stir in mushrooms and wine. Place a sausage in bone cavity of each thigh. On floured surface, roll each patty shell to a 6-inch square. Place thigh in center of each and top with 2 tablespoons sauce. Fold pastry over and seal; fold ends to center and seal. Place, seam side down, in 13½x8¾x1¾-inch baking dish. Brush with additional cream; bake at 400° till golden, 30 minutes. Heat remaining sauce; pass. Serves 6.

Roll thawed patty shells to 6-inch squares, then carefully wrap pastry around chicken and seal edges for *Chicken Vol-au-Vent.*

Chicken Liver-Sauced Pasta

Double the recipe and simmer the sauce in a Dutch oven to make 10 to 12 servings —

   ¼ cup chopped onion
   1 small clove garlic, minced
   4 tablespoons salad oil
   1 29-ounce can tomatoes, cut up
   1 6-ounce can tomato paste
   1 3-ounce can sliced mushrooms,
      drained
   2 tablespoons grated Parmesan cheese
   1½ teaspoons sugar
   ½ teaspoon dried oregano, crushed
   1 bay leaf
      Spaghetti or noodles
   1 pound chicken livers, cut up

In large saucepan cook onion and garlic in *2 tablespoons* oil till tender. Drain off fat. Stir in tomatoes, next 6 ingredients, ¾ cup water, ¾ teaspoon salt, and ⅛ teaspoon pepper. Simmer sauce, uncovered, for 45 minutes, stirring the mixture occasionally.

   Meanwhile, cook spaghetti or noodles in boiling, salted water just till tender; drain. Cook livers in remaining oil about 5 minutes, stirring gently; drain. Add livers to sauce; bring to boiling. Remove bay leaf. Spoon sauce atop each serving of pasta. Serves 5 or 6.

Wine-Glazed Hens

Cook and stir ¼ cup chopped onion and 2 tablespoons slivered almonds in 2 tablespoons butter or margarine about 5 minutes. Toss with 4 cups dry bread cubes; 2 medium oranges, peeled and diced; ¼ cup light raisins; and ½ teaspoon salt. Rinse six 1-pound ready-to-cook Rock Cornish game hens; pat dry. Season with salt and pepper. Lightly stuff birds with bread mixture. Skewer shut. Place hens, breast up, on rack in shallow roasting pan. Brush with salad oil; cover loosely. Roast at 375° for 30 minutes. Uncover; baste with Wine Glaze. Roast till done, about 1 hour more, basting frequently with glaze. (When done, drumstick can be twisted easily.) Makes 6 servings.

   Wine Glaze: Mix ½ cup Burgundy; ¼ cup butter, melted; and 2 tablespoons orange juice.

Layered Cherry-Cheese Mold

1 envelope unflavored gelatin
1 tablespoon lemon juice
1 3-ounce package cherry-flavored
    gelatin
¾ cup boiling water
1 tablespoon lemon juice
1 21-ounce can cherry pie filling
1 2-ounce package dessert topping mix
2 3-ounce packages cream cheese,
    softened

In saucepan soften unflavored gelatin in 1 cup cold water. Heat and stir till dissolved. Stir in 1 tablespoon lemon juice. Cool.

Meanwhile, dissolve cherry-flavored gelatin in the boiling water. Stir in the 1 tablespoon lemon juice and pie filling. Pour about ¼ of the cherry mixture into a 6½-cup mold. Chill till almost firm. Leave remainder of cherry mixture at room temperature.

Prepare dessert topping mix according to package directions. Beat in cream cheese. Fold in cooled unflavored gelatin. Spoon about ⅓ of white mixture over almost firm cherry layer. Chill till almost firm. Leave rest of white mixture at room temperature.

Top almost firm white layer with another ¼ of the cherry mixture. Chill till almost firm. (To hasten chilling, place in freezer for about 10 minutes. *Watch carefully* so that gelatin does not become too firm.) Repeat with remaining white and cherry mixtures, chilling after each layer and ending with cherry layer. Chill till firm. Makes 8 servings.

Creamy Fruit Salad

1 16-ounce can pear halves, chilled
1 8¾-ounce can pineapple tidbits,
    chilled
1 8¾-ounce can peach slices, chilled
    Lettuce cups
½ cup orange yogurt
1 tablespoon honey
⅛ teaspoon ground allspice

Drain fruits well; arrange in lettuce cups. Mix together yogurt, honey, and allspice. Serve over chilled fruits. Makes 6 servings.

Molded Cheese Ring

1 envelope unflavored gelatin
1½ cups cream-style cottage cheese
1 3-ounce package cream cheese,
    softened
⅓ cup chopped celery
1 tablespoon finely chopped green
    onion
½ cup milk
    Lettuce
    Fruit (grapefruit and orange sections,
    apricots, or plums)

Soften gelatin in ¼ cup cold water; place over hot water and stir to dissolve. Beat together cottage cheese and cream cheese till fluffy. (Some small lumps will remain.) Stir in celery, onion, and ¼ teaspoon salt. Stir in gelatin. Add milk; mix well. Chill till partially set. Turn into a 3-cup ring mold. Chill till firm. Unmold onto lettuce; pile fruit in center. Makes 4 to 6 servings.

Hearts of Palm Salad

¼ cup salad oil
1 tablespoon finely chopped onion
1 tablespoon snipped parsley
1 tablespoon vinegar
1 teaspoon lemon juice
⅛ teaspoon dry mustard
1 hard-cooked egg, finely chopped
1 tablespoon chopped canned pimiento
    Lettuce
1 14-ounce can hearts of palm, chilled,
    drained, and cut in strips

In screw-top jar combine first 6 ingredients and ¼ teaspoon salt. Cover; shake vigorously. Add chopped egg and pimiento; stir well. Line salad plates with lettuce; top with hearts of palm. Pour on dressing. Serves 4.

An elegant, layered beauty

Choose your prettiest 6½-cup mold for this →
Layered Cherry-Cheese Mold. Serve the salad on lettuce leaves for a colorful accent.

Zucchini Sweet-Sour Medley

A pretty red and green vegetable combo —

   2 tablespoons salad oil
   4 teaspoons cornstarch
   1 tablespoon sugar
   1 tablespoon instant minced onion
   2 teaspoons prepared mustard
   ¾ teaspoon salt
   ½ teaspoon garlic salt
     Dash pepper
   ½ cup water
   ¼ cup vinegar
      • • •
   4 cups bias-sliced zucchini
   1 cup bias-sliced celery
   2 tomatoes, quartered

In medium skillet stir together the first 8 ingredients. Add water and vinegar; cook and stir till thickened and bubbly. Add zucchini and celery. Cook, covered, till vegetables are crisp-tender, 7 to 8 minutes; stir occasionally. Add tomatoes; cook, covered, till heated through, 2 to 3 minutes. Serves 6.

Herbed Potato Fluff

Gourmet fare using instant mashed potatoes —

   Packaged instant mashed potatoes
     (enough for 4 servings)
   1 cup small curd cream-style cottage
     cheese
   ½ cup dairy sour cream
   3 egg yolks
   2 tablespoons snipped chives
   ½ teaspoon celery salt
   3 egg whites
   2 tablespoons finely snipped parsley
   2 tablespoons butter or margarine

Prepare mashed potatoes according to package directions. Beat in cottage cheese, sour cream, egg yolks, chives, and celery salt. Beat egg whites till stiff peaks form; fold into potato mixture along with the parsley. Turn into a 2-quart casserole; dot with butter or margarine. Bake at 350° till top is lightly browned, about 1 hour. Makes 6 to 8 servings.

Special Broccoli Casserole

Double the recipe and bake in a 13x9x2-inch baking pan about 35 minutes for 12 servings —

   1 10-ounce package frozen
     broccoli cuts
   1 10½-ounce can condensed cream of
     mushroom soup
   2 ounces sharp process American
     cheese, shredded (½ cup)
   ¼ cup milk
   ¼ cup mayonnaise
   1 beaten egg
   ¼ cup fine dry bread crumbs
   1 tablespoon butter, melted

Cook broccoli according to package directions, omitting salt called for; drain thoroughly. Place broccoli in 10x6x1¾-inch baking dish. Stir together soup and cheese; gradually add milk, mayonnaise, and egg, stirring to blend. Pour over broccoli. Combine crumbs and melted butter; sprinkle over soup mixture. Bake at 350° till heated and crumbs are lightly browned, about 35 minutes. Serves 6.

Corn-Stuffed Onions

   6 medium onions
   1 12-ounce can whole kernel corn,
     drained
   2 tablespoons butter or margarine
   2 tablespoons all-purpose flour
   ½ teaspoon salt
     Dash pepper
   1 cup milk
   2 tablespoons chopped canned pimiento
   4 ounces process American cheese,
     shredded (1 cup)

Hollow the onions; chop centers to make 1 cup. Fill onions with corn; set aside remaining corn. Place onions in 9x9x2-inch baking pan. Add 2 tablespoons water; cover. Bake at 400° for 1 hour. Cook chopped onion in butter; stir in flour, salt, and pepper. Add milk; cook and stir till thickened. Add reserved corn and pimiento. Return to bubbling; stir in cheese till melted. Place onions in serving dish; spoon sauce over. Makes 6 servings.

Combine two vegetable favorites in one dish by serving *Corn-Stuffed Onions*. Bake the corn-filled onions, and then at serving time spoon on the flavorful cheese sauce.

Asparagus Divan

    2 pounds asparagus spears, cooked
    3 hard-cooked eggs, sliced
    1 8¾-ounce can ready-to-serve
        hollandaise sauce
    ¼ cup frozen whipped dessert
        topping, thawed
    1 teaspoon lemon juice
    1 teaspoon grated lemon peel

Drain asparagus. Arrange hot asparagus in ovenproof dish. Top with egg slices. Blend together hollandaise sauce, whipped topping, and lemon juice; spoon atop asparagus and eggs. Broil 3 to 4 inches from heat till top is lightly browned, 6 to 8 minutes. Sprinkle with lemon peel. Makes 6 to 8 servings.

Blender Hollandaise

    3 egg yolks
    2 tablespoons lemon juice
    ½ teaspoon prepared mustard
        Dash cayenne
    ½ cup butter or margarine

Put first 4 ingredients in blender container; blend till ingredients are combined. Heat butter in saucepan till melted and almost boiling. With blender slowly running, slowly pour about a *third* of the hot butter, in a thin stream, into the blender container. Turn blender to high speed; slowly pour in remaining hot butter, blending till mixture is smooth and thickened. Serve immediately over hot cooked vegetables. Makes 1 cup.

Caraway Puffs

An easy no-knead roll—

1 package active dry yeast
2⅓ cups sifted all-purpose flour
¼ teaspoon baking soda
1 cup cream-style cottage cheese
2 tablespoons sugar
1 tablespoon butter or margarine
1 teaspoon salt
1 egg
2 teaspoons caraway seed
2 teaspoons grated onion

In mixer bowl combine yeast, *1⅓ cups* of the flour, and the baking soda. Heat together cottage cheese, ¼ cup water, sugar, butter, and salt till butter melts; add to dry ingredients. Add egg, caraway seed, and onion. Beat at low speed of electric mixer for ½ minute. Beat 3 minutes at high speed. Stir in remaining flour. Place in greased bowl, turning once. Cover; let rise till double, 1½ hours. Divide among 12 well-greased muffin pans. Cover; let rise about 40 minutes. Bake at 400° for 12 to 15 minutes. Makes 12.

Biscuits Supreme

Best when served piping hot—

2 cups sifted all-purpose flour
4 teaspoons baking powder
½ teaspoon salt
½ teaspoon cream of tartar
2 teaspoons sugar
½ cup shortening
⅔ cup milk

Sift together flour, baking powder, salt, cream of tartar, and sugar in bowl. Cut in shortening till like coarse crumbs. Make a well; add milk all at once. Stir quickly with a fork, just till dough follows fork around bowl. Turn onto lightly floured surface. (Dough should be soft.) Knead gently 10 to 12 strokes. Roll or pat dough ½ inch thick. Dip biscuit cutter in flour; cut dough straight down. Bake on ungreased baking sheet at 450° for 10 to 12 minutes. Makes about 16 biscuits.

Apricot-Almond Coffee Cake

¾ cup dried apricots, snipped
1 cup water
Milk
¼ cup shortening
¾ cup granulated sugar
1 egg
1½ cups sifted all-purpose flour
2 teaspoons baking powder
¾ teaspoon salt
½ teaspoon ground cinnamon
½ cup brown sugar
⅓ cup sifted all-purpose flour
¼ cup butter or margarine
⅓ cup chopped almonds

In saucepan combine snipped apricots and water; simmer, uncovered, 15 minutes. Cool. Drain, reserving liquid. Add enough milk to liquid to make ½ cup. Cream together shortening and granulated sugar. Add egg; beat well. Sift together the 1½ cups flour, the baking powder, salt, and cinnamon. Add to creamed mixture alternately with milk mixture, beginning and ending with dry ingredients; stir in apricots. Turn into greased 9x1½-inch round cake pan *or* 9x9x2-inch baking pan.

Combine brown sugar and the ⅓ cup flour. Cut in butter or margarine till crumbly; add almonds. Sprinkle over batter in pan. Bake at 350° for 40 to 45 minutes. Serve warm.

Peanut Bread

1¾ cups sifted all-purpose flour
½ cup sugar
2½ teaspoons baking powder
½ cup creamy peanut butter
¾ cup milk
2 beaten eggs
½ cup chopped peanuts

In mixing bowl sift together flour, sugar, baking powder, and ½ teaspoon salt. Cut in peanut butter till mixture is crumbly. Add milk and eggs all at once, stirring just till mixture is well combined. Stir in peanuts. Turn batter into well-greased 9x5x3-inch loaf pan. Bake at 350° for 40 to 45 minutes. Remove from pan; cool on rack. Makes 1 loaf.

Fig-Oatmeal Muffins

1 cup sifted all-purpose flour
¼ cup sugar
3 teaspoons baking powder
1 cup quick-cooking rolled oats
½ cup chopped dried figs
1 beaten egg
1 cup milk
3 tablespoons salad oil

Sift together first 3 ingredients and ½ teaspoon salt. Stir in rolled oats and figs. Add egg, milk, and oil; stir just till moistened. Fill greased muffin pans ⅔ full. Bake at 425° for 15 to 17 minutes. Makes 12 muffins.

Easy Bread Fix-Ups

Dilly Bread: In small mixing bowl combine ¼ cup softened butter or margarine, ½ teaspoon prepared mustard, and ¼ teaspoon dried dillweed, crushed. Spread butter mixture on one side of 8 slices French bread. Place, buttered side down, on baking sheet. Broil till golden, 1 to 2 minutes. Turn and broil 1 to 2 minutes more. Makes 8 slices.

Parsley-Onion Bread: In small mixing bowl combine 1 tablespoon instant minced onion and 1 tablespoon milk. Stir in ¼ cup softened butter and 2 tablespoons snipped parsley. Spread butter mixture on one side of 8 slices French bread. Place, buttered side down, on baking sheet. Broil 1 to 2 minutes. Turn; broil 1 to 2 minutes more. Makes 8 slices.

Cheesy Biscuits: In small mixing bowl combine *half* of a 5-ounce jar Neufchatel cheese spread with pimiento (⅓ cup) and 2 tablespoons softened butter. Using 1 tube refrigerated biscuits (10), spread biscuits with cheese mixture. Bake on baking sheet at 425° about 15 minutes. Makes 10 biscuits.

Sesame-Garlic Crisps: Cut 3 sliced hamburger buns in half vertically. Then, cut each piece in half again horizontally (for a total of 24 half-rounds). Combine ¼ cup softened butter and ½ teaspoon garlic powder. Spread one side of each bun piece with butter mixture. Place, buttered side up, on baking sheet. Sprinkle with 2 tablespoons sesame seed. Bake at 425° till golden, 8 to 10 minutes. Makes 24.

Impress guests at any meal by serving *Caraway Puffs* with whipped butter. Not only are they good to eat, they are easy to fix. Try them.

Immediately after pouring *Peach Crepes* batter into a hot, greased skillet or crepe pan, rotate the pan to spread the batter evenly.

Dreamy-High Pumpkin Pie

     1 cup sugar
     1 envelope unflavored gelatin
     1 teaspoon ground cinnamon
     ¼ teaspoon ground nutmeg
     3 slightly beaten egg yolks
     ¾ cup milk
     1 cup cooked or canned pumpkin
     3 egg whites
        Graham Cracker Crust
     ½ cup whipping cream
     ½ cup flaked coconut

In saucepan mix ⅔ *cup* sugar, gelatin, cinnamon, ½ teaspoon salt, and nutmeg. Combine egg yolks and milk; add to gelatin mixture. Cook and stir till slightly thickened. Stir in pumpkin. Chill till mixture mounds slightly when spooned, stirring often. Beat egg whites till soft peaks form. Gradually add remaining sugar, beating to stiff peaks. Fold pumpkin mixture into whites. Pile into Graham Cracker Crust. Chill till firm. Whip cream; spoon atop pie. Sprinkle with coconut.

Graham Cracker Crust: Combine 1¼ cups fine graham cracker crumbs, ¼ cup sugar, and 6 tablespoons butter, melted; mix. Press firmly into 9-inch pie plate. Bake at 375° till edges are browned, 6 to 8 minutes; cool.

Peach Crepes

     1 cup sifted all-purpose flour
     1 tablespoon sugar
     ⅛ teaspoon salt
     2 eggs
     1½ cups milk
        Creamy Filling
     ¼ cup finely chopped pecans
     1 29-ounce can peach slices
     2 tablespoons cornstarch
     ½ cup orange juice
     2 tablespoons lemon juice
     2 tablespoons butter or margarine
     ¼ cup orange-flavored liqueur

In mixing bowl combine first 5 ingredients; beat till mixture is smooth. Lightly grease a 6-inch skillet or crepe pan; heat. Remove pan from heat; spoon in about 2 tablespoons batter. Rotate pan so batter spreads evenly. Return to heat; brown on one side only. To remove, invert pan over paper toweling. Repeat with remaining batter to make 16 crepes, lightly greasing pan occasionally.

Prepare Creamy Filling. Spread unbrowned side of each crepe with Creamy Filling; sprinkle with pecans. Fold in quarters.

Drain peach slices, reserving syrup. In blazer pan of chafing dish, gradually blend reserved syrup into cornstarch. Add orange juice, lemon juice, and butter. Cook and stir over direct heat till thickened and bubbly. Add peaches and crepes. Spoon sauce over crepes; heat through. Set pan over hot water (bain-marie). Warm liqueur in small saucepan. Pour over crepes; ignite liqueur. Serves 8.

Creamy Filling: Beat together two 3-ounce packages cream cheese, softened; 3 tablespoons sugar; 2 tablespoons milk; ½ teaspoon shredded orange peel; and ¼ teaspoon vanilla.

Orange-Date Medley

Peel and section 5 oranges. Place oranges and 1 cup sliced dates in a 10x6x1¾-inch baking dish. Combine 1 cup orange juice and 2 tablespoons orange-flavored liqueur; pour over fruit. Bake, covered, at 350° till heated through, about 30 minutes. Sprinkle ¼ cup toasted slivered almonds atop. Serves 6.

Pear Chiffon Pie

A light meal ending—

>   1 29-ounce can pear halves
>   ⅓ cup sugar
>   1 envelope unflavored gelatin
>   ¼ teaspoon salt
>   3 slightly beaten egg yolks
>   ¼ teaspoon grated lemon peel
>   1 tablespoon lemon juice
>   3 egg whites
>   ⅓ cup sugar
>   1 *baked* 9-inch pastry shell, cooled
>   Whipped cream

Drain pears, reserving ¼ cup syrup and 1 pear half. With fork, mash remaining pear halves; drain. Combine ⅓ cup sugar, gelatin, and salt; stir in reserved pear syrup, egg yolks, lemon peel, and lemon juice. Cook and stir till slightly thickened. Add mashed pears. Cool till mixture mounds. Beat egg whites to soft peaks; gradually add ⅓ cup sugar, beating till stiff peaks form. Fold in pear mixture. Turn into baked pastry shell; chill. Garnish with dollops of whipped cream and the reserved pear half, sliced.

Irish Coffee Pie

Delicately flavored with Irish whiskey—

>   1 3½-ounce package vanilla whipped
>   dessert mix
>   2 teaspoons instant coffee powder
>   ½ cup cold milk
>   3 tablespoons Irish whiskey
>   ½ cup whipping cream
>   1 *baked* 8-inch pastry shell, cooled

In small mixer bowl combine dessert mix and instant coffee powder. Add milk; beat at high speed of electric mixer about 1 minute. Blend in ⅓ cup water and Irish whiskey; beat at high speed till fluffy, about 2 minutes more. Whip cream; carefully fold into prepared filling. Pile into baked pastry shell and chill for 3 to 4 hours. Garnish each serving with additional whipped cream and chocolate shavings, if desired.

Pastry Shell

Sift together 1½ cups sifted all-purpose flour and ½ teaspoon salt; cut in ½ cup shortening with pastry blender till pieces are the size of small peas. Sprinkle 1 tablespoon cold water over mixture. Gently toss with fork; push to side of bowl. Repeat, using 3 to 4 tablespoons more cold water, till all is moist. Form into ball. Flatten on lightly floured surface by pressing with edge of hand 3 times across in both directions. Roll from center to edge till pastry is ⅛ inch thick.

Fit pastry into pie plate. Trim ½ to 1 inch beyond edge. Fold under; flute edge by pressing dough with forefinger against wedge made of finger and thumb of other hand. Prick bottom and sides well. (If filling and crust are baked together, *do not prick.*) Bake at 450° till golden, 10 to 12 minutes.

Delight guests with light, fluffy *Irish Coffee Pie,* specially flavored with a combination of instant coffee powder and Irish whiskey.

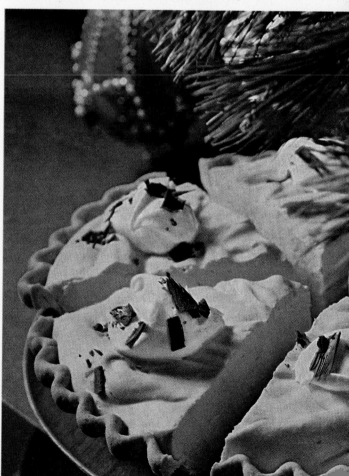

Forgotten Cherry Torte

    5 egg whites
    ½ teaspoon cream of tartar
    ¼ teaspoon salt
    1½ cups sugar
    2 cups frozen whipped dessert
        topping, thawed
    1 21-ounce can cherry pie filling
    1 tablespoon lemon juice
        Several drops almond extract

Preheat oven to 450°. In mixer bowl beat egg whites till frothy. Add cream of tartar and salt; beat till soft peaks form. Gradually add sugar, a tablespoon at a time, beating till stiff peaks form. Turn into buttered 8x8x2-inch baking dish; smooth with spatula. Place in preheated oven. *Close oven door; immediately turn off heat. Leave oven door closed for 8 hours or overnight.* (Don't peek!)

Spread *half* the whipped topping over meringue. Combine pie filling, lemon juice, and extract; spread *half* over topping in baking dish. Repeat layers with topping and cherry mixture, spreading to cover edges. Cover; chill overnight. Cut in squares; top with whipped topping, if desired. Serves 6 to 8.

Strawberry-Vanilla Pudding

    4½ to 5 cups angel cake cubes
        (6 ounces)
    1 3- or 3¾-ounce package *instant*
        vanilla pudding mix
    1 cup cold milk
    1 pint vanilla ice cream, softened
    1 3-ounce package strawberry-
        flavored gelatin
    1½ cups boiling water
    1 10-ounce package frozen strawberry
        slices

Place angel cake cubes in 9x9x2-inch baking pan. In mixer bowl combine instant pudding and milk; add ice cream. Beat at low speed till well blended. Pour over cake cubes. Chill till firm. Dissolve gelatin in boiling water; add frozen berries. Stir till gelatin begins to thicken. Pour over pudding; do not stir. Chill till set. Makes 8 or 9 servings.

Elegant Chocolate Soufflé

Serve hot right from the oven —

    3 tablespoons butter or margarine
    ¼ cup all-purpose flour
    1 cup milk
    2 1-ounce squares unsweetened
        chocolate, cut up
    4 egg yolks
    ½ cup sugar
    4 egg whites
    ¼ teaspoon cream of tartar
        Grand Marnier Sauce

In saucepan melt butter; blend in flour and ¼ teaspoon salt. Add milk; cook and stir till thickened and bubbly. Add chocolate; stir till melted. Remove from heat. Beat yolks till thick and lemon-colored. Beat sugar into yolks gradually. Blend chocolate mixture into yolk mixture. Beat whites and cream of tartar till stiff peaks form. Carefully fold whites into chocolate mixture. Pour into ungreased 5-cup soufflé dish with foil collar. (Measure a length of foil to go around dish; fold in thirds. Butter well; sprinkle with sugar. Extend collar 2 inches above dish; fasten with tape.) Bake at 325° for 60 to 70 minutes. Serve with Grand Marnier Sauce. Serves 5 or 6.

Grand Marnier Sauce: In saucepan combine ¼ cup sugar and 1 tablespoon cornstarch; stir in ¾ cup orange juice. Cook and stir till thickened and bubbly. Add ¼ cup Grand Marnier liqueur and ¼ cup toasted slivered almonds.

Jade Cream Mold

    1 2- or 2⅛-ounce package dessert
        topping mix
    1 quart vanilla ice cream, softened
    1 pint lime sherbet, softened
    ¼ cup green creme de menthe
        Chocolate curls

Prepare topping mix according to package directions. Stir together ice cream, sherbet, creme de menthe, and whipped topping; turn into one 6-cup mold or two 3-cup refrigerator trays. Freeze. To serve, unmold and garnish with chocolate curls. Makes 6 to 8 servings.

Nesselrode Mold

1 10¾- or 11-ounce package no-bake
    cheesecake mix
3 tablespoons sugar
¼ cup butter or margarine, melted
½ cup chopped mixed candied fruits
    and peels
⅓ cup chopped pecans
3 tablespoons dry sherry
1⅓ cups cold milk
½ cup whipping cream

Combine crust mix from cheesecake mix, *2
tablespoons* sugar, and the melted butter or
margarine. Press firmly against bottom and
sides of 4-cup mold. Chill. Combine fruits and
peels, pecans, and sherry; set aside. Pour milk
into small mixer bowl; add cheesecake filling
mix and remaining sugar. Beat at low speed
of electric mixer till blended. Beat at high
speed till thickened, 3 minutes. Whip cream;
fold into cheesecake mixture along with
candied fruit mixture. Pour into mold; freeze.
Unmold; let stand at room temperature 5
minutes. Garnish with spiced whipped cream
and candied fruits, if desired. Serves 6 to 8.

Chocolate Fondue

8 1-ounce squares semisweet
    chocolate
1 15-ounce can *sweetened condensed*
    milk (1⅓ cups)
⅓ cup milk
2 tablespoons instant coffee powder
    or 4 ounces cream-filled mint
    patties *or* ¼ cup brandy *or* ⅓
    cup orange-flavored liqueur
    Cookies, angel cake squares,
    banana or pineapple chunks

In saucepan melt chocolate; stir in sweetened
condensed milk and regular milk till well
blended. Heat through. Stir in coffee powder,
mint patties, brandy, *or* liqueur. Pour into
fondue pot. Place over fondue burner. (If
desired, thin fondue with more milk; fondue
will thicken as it stands.) Use as dip for cookies,
angel cake, banana or pineapple chunks, or
other fruits. Makes 2½ cups sauce.

Select either orange-flavored liqueur, coffee,
mint, or brandy to add an unusual flavor to
this creamy rich *Chocolate Fondue*.

Lemon Fluff Squares

*Double the recipe and place in a 13x9x2-inch
baking pan to make 16 servings—*

1½ cups finely crushed vanilla wafers
⅓ cup chopped pecans
6 tablespoons butter, melted
2 3-ounce packages or 1 6-ounce
    package lemon-flavored gelatin
1¼ cups boiling water
½ cup whipping cream
1 3¾- or 3⅝-ounce package *instant*
    lemon pudding mix
1 pint lemon sherbet, softened

Combine crumbs, pecans, and butter. Reserve
½ cup mixture; press remainder into a 10x6x
1¾-inch baking dish. Chill. Dissolve gelatin in
boiling water; cool. Whip cream till soft peaks
form; set aside. Add pudding mix to gelatin;
mix well. Add sherbet; beat at low speed of
electric mixer till thickened and nearly set.
Fold in whipped cream. Turn into baking
dish; sprinkle reserved crumbs atop. Chill at
least 1 hour. Makes 8 servings.

Strawberries Romanoff

An elegant, yet simple dessert—

  1½ pints fresh strawberries, hulled
      and sliced
   ⅓ cup orange-flavored liqueur
   2 tablespoons sugar
   ½ cup whipping cream
   2 tablespoons sugar
   1 teaspoon vanilla
     Shredded orange peel

Combine strawberries, liqueur, and 2 tablespoons sugar; chill at least 2 hours. Whip
cream with 2 tablespoons sugar and vanilla
just till soft peaks form. Spoon berries and
liquid into sherbet dishes; top with whipped
cream. Garnish with orange peel. Serves 4.

Peach Posies

   1 16-ounce can peach slices
   1 3-ounce package cream cheese,
     softened
   ¼ cup sifted confectioners' sugar
       • • •
   1 8-ounce can date-nut roll
   2 tablespoons chopped maraschino
     cherries

Drain peaches, reserving 2 teaspoons syrup.
In small bowl blend softened cream cheese and
reserved peach syrup. Stir in confectioners'
sugar; mix well. Cut the date-nut roll into
6 slices. For each serving, place a few peach
slices on each cake slice. Top with a spoonful
of the cream cheese mixture. Garnish with a
few chopped cherries. Makes 6 servings.

Easy Date Crumble Torte, a company-special
dessert, starts with a package of date bar mix.

To this, add walnuts, butter, and whipped
topping. To serve, top with walnut halves.

Mai Tai Banana Mold

A light, refreshing meal ending—

½ cup sugar
1 envelope unflavored gelatin
Dash salt
2 beaten egg yolks
½ cup pineapple juice
¾ cup bottled nonalcoholic mai tai
cocktail mix

• • •

2 egg whites
2 tablespoons sugar
½ cup whipping cream
3 medium bananas

In saucepan combine ½ cup sugar, gelatin, and salt. Stir in egg yolks; mix well. Blend in pineapple juice. Cook and stir till mixture thickens and gelatin is dissolved. Stir in mai tai mix. Chill till partially set. Beat egg whites to soft peaks. Gradually add 2 tablespoons sugar; beat to stiff peaks. Whip cream. Fold beaten egg whites into gelatin mixture; fold in whipped cream. Chill till mixture mounds. Slice bananas; fold into gelatin mixture. Turn into 5-cup mold. Chill till firm. Serves 6 to 8.

Easy Date Crumble Torte

1 14-ounce package date bar mix
½ cup chopped walnuts
2 tablespoons butter or margarine,
melted
1 cup frozen whipped dessert topping,
thawed
Walnut halves

Combine the crumb portion of the date bar mix and chopped walnuts; stir in melted butter or margarine. Mix well. Spread in a 13x9x2-inch baking pan. Bake at 400° for 10 minutes. Break up with a fork; cool and crumble.

Prepare date filling following package directions; cool. Place *half* the crumb mixture in bottom of 10x6x1¾-inch baking dish. Cover with *half* the dessert topping, then with date mixture. Repeat crumb and whipped topping layers. Chill several hours. Top each serving with a walnut half. Serves 8.

Chocolate-Mint Cups

No last-minute preparation needed—

1 cup slightly crushed, crisp rice
cereal
⅓ cup flaked coconut
¼ cup finely chopped walnuts
1 6-ounce package semisweet
chocolate pieces (1 cup)
Peppermint ice cream

In medium mixing bowl toss together crushed cereal, coconut, and walnuts; set aside. In heavy saucepan heat and stir chocolate pieces till melted. Remove from heat; stir in cereal mixture. Press about ⅓ cup mixture firmly onto bottom and sides of greased, deep muffin pan (or paper bake cup in muffin pan) to form a shell. Repeat with remaining cereal mixture, making 6 shells in all. Chill till shells are firm. Fill each shell with a large scoop of peppermint ice cream. Cover lightly and freeze firm. Remove from freezer a few minutes before serving. Carefully remove each filled shell from muffin pan. Makes 6 servings.

Cupcake Alaskas

Fill cupcakes with your favorite ice cream—

4 large chocolate cupcakes
2 egg whites
⅛ teaspoon cream of tartar
¼ teaspoon vanilla
Dash salt
¼ cup sugar
Ice cream (butter brickle, pistachio,
butter pecan, or cherry-nut)

Hollow out center of cupcakes, leaving about ¼ inch of cake around sides and bottom. Beat egg whites with cream of tartar, vanilla, and salt till soft peaks form. Gradually add sugar, beating to stiff peaks. Fill cupcakes with ice cream and place on wooden cutting board. Quickly cover top and sides with meringue, sealing edges at bottom. Place Alaskas in freezer. At serving time, bake Alaskas at 500° till meringue is browned, 2 to 3 minutes. Serve immediately. Serves 4.

MENUS

WEEKEND BREAKFAST (4)

Fruit Skewers *or* Gala Grapefruit
Puffy Omelet
with
Cheese-Mushroom Sauce
Smoked Sausage Links
Spicy Marble Coffee Cake
Coffee   Milk

Start off the weekend right by serving overnight guests a hearty breakfast. Serve the first course, either a hot or cold fruit dish, while the omelet is in the oven. Then, ease out the Puffy Omelet onto a warmed plate and cover with smooth Cheese-Mushroom Sauce. Accompany with smoked sausages and still-warm coffee cake. You can then leisurely enjoy the delicious food along with your guests.

Fruit Skewers

1 20½-ounce can pineapple chunks
¼ cup honey
1 tablespoon brandy
1 teaspoon snipped fresh mint or
 dried mint flakes
1 apple, cut into wedges and cored
1 pear, cut into wedges and cored
1 nectarine, pitted and cut into
 wedges

Drain pineapple chunks, reserving syrup. To reserved syrup add honey, brandy, and fresh or dried mint. Place pineapple, apple, pear, and nectarine pieces in shallow dish; add honey mixture. Marinate in refrigerator at least 2 to 3 hours, turning wedges occasionally. Drain and thread on skewers, *or* serve in sherbets with marinade. Makes 4 servings.

Puffy Omelet

4 egg whites
4 egg yolks
1 tablespoon butter or margarine

Beat whites till frothy; add 2 tablespoons water and ¼ teaspoon salt. Beat till stiff peaks form. Beat yolks till very thick and lemon-colored. Fold yolks into whites. Melt butter in 10-inch ovenproof skillet; heat till drop of water sizzles. Pour in egg mixture; spread to edges of skillet, leaving higher at sides. Reduce heat; cook till puffed and bottom is golden, 7 to 8 minutes. Bake at 325° till knife inserted in center comes out clean, about 8 minutes. Loosen sides of omelet. Make shallow cut across omelet, slightly off-center and parallel to skillet handle. Tilt pan; fold upper (smaller) half over lower half. Slip onto warm plate. Makes 4 servings.

When knife inserted in center comes out clean, remove omelet from oven. Fold carefully; slip onto warm plate. Serve quickly.

Cheese-Mushroom Sauce

 1 tablespoon butter or margarine
 1 tablespoon all-purpose flour
 ¼ teaspoon salt
   Dash pepper
 ¾ cup milk
 3 ounces sharp process American
   cheese, shredded (¾ cup)
 1 3-ounce can sliced mushrooms,
   drained

In saucepan melt butter over low heat. Blend in flour, salt, and pepper. Add milk all at once. Cook quickly, stirring constantly, till thickened and bubbly. Add cheese; stir till smooth. Remove from heat; stir in mushrooms. Serve over hot omelet. Makes 1¼ cups.

Spicy Marble Coffee Cake

 ½ cup shortening
 ¾ cup granulated sugar
 1 egg
 2 cups sifted all-purpose flour
 2 teaspoons baking powder
 ½ teaspoon salt
 ¾ cup milk
 2 tablespoons light molasses
 ½ teaspoon ground cinnamon
 ¼ teaspoon ground nutmeg
 ⅛ teaspoon ground cloves
 ½ cup brown sugar
 ¼ cup chopped walnuts
 2 tablespoons all-purpose flour
 1 teaspoon ground cinnamon
 2 tablespoons butter or margarine,
   melted

Cream together shortening and granulated sugar. Add egg; beat well. Sift together 2 cups flour, baking powder, and salt. Add to creamed mixture alternately with milk, beating after each addition. Divide batter in half. To one half, add molasses, ½ teaspoon cinnamon, nutmeg, and cloves; mix well. Spoon batters alternately into greased 9x9x2-inch baking pan. Zigzag batter with spatula to marble. Combine remaining ingredients; mix well. Sprinkle atop batter. Bake at 350° for 35 to 40 minutes. Serve warm.

Gala Grapefruit

 2 medium grapefruit
 3 tablespoons brown sugar
 4 teaspoons rum flavoring
 4 teaspoons butter or margarine
 ¼ cup flaked coconut
   Maraschino cherries

Halve the grapefruit, making zigzag edge. With a knife, cut around each section to loosen from membrane. Sprinkle *each* grapefruit half with about 2 teaspoons of the brown sugar and 1 teaspoon rum flavoring. Dot with butter or margarine; sprinkle coconut atop. Bake at 400° for 20 minutes. Garnish with maraschino cherries. Makes 4 servings.

Satisfy everyone's morning appetite with minty *Fruit Skewers, Spicy Marble Coffee Cake, Puffy Omelet,* and smoked sausage links.

Take advantage of warm weather by having a brunch on the patio. Combine breakfast and lunch into one meal featuring breakfast steaks, grilled tomatoes, a cold juice beverage, either alcoholic or nonalcoholic, and coffee cake. For real convenience, cook the steaks and heat the fresh tomato wedges on a portable griddle plugged into an outdoor outlet.

Marinated Breakfast Steaks

Subtly flavored with a wine-soy marinade—

¾ cup salad oil
½ cup sauterne
⅓ cup soy sauce
1 clove garlic, minced
½ teaspoon ground ginger
½ teaspoon paprika
   Dash pepper
• • •
6 ¼- to ½-inch thick breakfast
   steaks cut from beef round,
   sirloin tip, or shoulder
   (about 3 ounces each)
   Sliced mushrooms (optional)

In small mixing bowl combine salad oil, sauterne, soy sauce, minced garlic, ground ginger, paprika, and pepper; mix well. Pour over steaks in shallow pan or dish. Let stand for 1½ hours in refrigerator. Drain; cook steaks on greased electric griddle or skillet for 1 to 1½ minutes on each side. Garnish with grilled mushrooms, if desired. Makes 6 servings.

Coconut Coffee Cake

Serve with butter balls—

1 package active dry yeast
2 to 2¼ cups sifted all-purpose flour
½ cup milk
¼ cup sugar
¼ cup butter or margarine
½ teaspoon salt
1 egg
• • •
¼ cup flaked coconut
¼ cup sugar
1 tablespoon butter or margarine,
   melted
   Coconut Topping
   Confectioners' Icing

In small mixer bowl combine yeast and *1 cup* of the flour. Heat milk, ¼ cup sugar, ¼ cup butter, and salt just till warm, stirring occasionally to melt butter. Add to dry mixture in mixer bowl; add egg. Beat at low speed with electric mixer for ½ minute, scraping sides of bowl constantly. Beat 3 minutes at high speed. By hand, stir in enough of the remaining flour to make a moderately stiff dough. Turn out on lightly floured surface; knead 3 to 5 minutes. Place in greased bowl, turning once to grease surface. Cover; let rise in warm place till double, about 1 hour.

Combine coconut and ¼ cup sugar. Turn dough out on floured surface. Cover and let rest 10 minutes. Roll dough to a 12x8-inch rectangle. Brush with 1 tablespoon melted butter. Sprinkle with coconut-sugar mixture. Roll up, starting with long side. Cut into 12 1-inch slices. Place, cut side down, in greased 9x1½-inch round baking pan. Sprinkle Coconut Topping over coffee cake. Let rise in warm place till double, about 30 minutes. Bake at 350° till golden brown, 25 to 30 minutes. Remove from pan and cool right side up. Drizzle Confectioners' Icing over cooled coffee cake.

Coconut Topping: In small mixing bowl mix ¼ cup all-purpose flour, 2 tablespoons brown sugar, and 2 tablespoons granulated sugar. Cut in 2 tablespoons butter or margarine till mixture is crumbly. Add ¼ cup flaked coconut.

Confectioners' Icing: Combine ½ cup sifted confectioners' sugar and 2 teaspoons milk.

Orange-Apricot Nog

Made in a jiffy in the blender—

1 orange, peeled and cut into
   small pieces
1 16-ounce can apricot halves,
   undrained and chilled
1 egg
½ cup cold milk
1 teaspoon vanilla

Blend orange and undrained apricots in
blender till smooth. Add egg, milk, and vanilla.
Blend 1 minute. Serve immediately. Serves 6.

Orange-Champagne Cocktail

Fresh strawberry slices make a pretty garnish—

1 4/5-pint bottle champagne, chilled
   (1¾ cups)
2 7-ounce bottles ginger ale, chilled
   (about 2 cups)
1 cup orange juice, chilled
   Strawberries, washed, hulled,
   and sliced

Combine champagne, ginger ale, and orange
juice in pitcher; stir gently. Serve with a few
strawberry slices in glasses. Serves 6.

Let brunch guests help themselves to juicy
Marinated Breakfast Steaks and grilled toma-
toes hot off the griddle, rich *Coconut Coffee
Cake,* and *Orange-Champagne Cocktail.*

```
┌─────────────────────────────────┐
│       SUMMER LUNCHEON (8)        │
│                                  │
│         Tomato Juice             │
│      Deviled Beef Salad          │
│        Bacon Popovers            │
│  Ice Cream    Choco-Peanut Sauce │
│           Iced Tea               │
└─────────────────────────────────┘
```

For a pleasant change from hot main dishes, serve warm-weather luncheon guests individual main dish tossed salads. Accompany the generous salads with just-from-the-oven popovers. To round out this simple, yet delicious meal, serve a juice appetizer, an ice cream-chocolate sauce dessert, and a cold beverage.

Bacon Popovers

A traditional quick bread with extra flavor—

>   4 slices bacon
>   2 eggs
>   1 cup milk
>   1 cup sifted all-purpose flour
>   ½ teaspoon salt
>   • • •
>   ½ cup butter or margarine, softened
>   ⅛ teaspoon dried oregano, crushed
>   ⅛ teaspoon dried sage, crushed

Cook bacon till crisp; drain, reserving 1 tablespoon drippings. Crumble bacon finely; set aside. In mixer bowl combine eggs and milk; add flour and salt. Beat 1½ minutes with rotary beater or electric mixer. Add reserved bacon drippings; beat 30 seconds. (Don't overbeat.) Stir in bacon. Fill 8 greased custard cups half full. Bake at 475° for 15 minutes. Without removing popovers from oven, reduce heat to 350°; continue baking till popovers are browned and firm, about 25 to 30 minutes more. Meanwhile, cream together butter or margarine, crushed oregano, and sage. Prick popovers with fork before removing from oven. Serve hot with herb butter. Makes 8.

Deviled Beef Salad

Horseradish adds zip to the dressing—

>   1 tablespoon sugar
>   1 teaspoon dry mustard
>   ¼ teaspoon white pepper
>   Dash paprika
>   2 teaspoons prepared horseradish
>   ½ teaspoon grated onion
>   ⅔ cup salad oil
>   ⅓ cup white wine vinegar
>   1½ pounds beef top sirloin steak,
>   cut 1 inch thick
>   1 head romaine, torn in pieces
>   1 medium head iceberg lettuce, torn
>   in pieces
>   2 cups cherry tomatoes, halved
>   ½ medium onion, sliced and separated
>   into rings
>   1 2-ounce can rolled anchovy fillets
>   2 hard-cooked eggs, sliced

To make dressing mix sugar, mustard, ½ teaspoon salt, pepper, and paprika in small mixer bowl. Add horseradish and grated onion. Beating constantly with electric mixer at medium-high speed, slowly add oil, a little at a time, alternately with wine vinegar. Chill.

Broil steak 3 inches from heat till medium-rare, about 7 minutes per side; cool. Slice steak into thin strips; chill. In large bowl toss romaine and iceberg lettuce; divide among 8 individual salad bowls. Arrange steak strips, tomatoes, onion rings, anchovies, and egg atop greens. Drizzle with dressing. Serves 8.

Choco-Peanut Sauce

Be sure to serve this warm—

>   1 6-ounce package semisweet chocolate
>   pieces
>   1 cup milk
>   ½ cup peanut butter
>   ⅓ cup coarsely chopped peanuts

In saucepan combine chocolate and milk. Cook and stir till chocolate is melted. Stir in peanut butter; mix well. Stir in peanuts. Serve warm over ice cream. Makes 1¾ cups.

```
┌─────────────────────────────────┐
│     MAKE-AHEAD LUNCH (6)         │
│                                  │
│     Cheesy Chicken Strata        │
│       Buttered Broccoli          │
│     Tomato Salad Special         │
│      Elegant Fruit Medley        │
│   Coffee            Iced Tea     │
└─────────────────────────────────┘
```

Company coming? Then why not prepare a luncheon that requires very little last-minute preparation? Fix the main dish, most of the salad, and the dessert a day ahead. Then, starting about an hour before guests arrive, slip the chicken casserole in the oven, finish the salad, set the table, prepare the beverage, and put the vegetable on to cook.

Cheesy Chicken Strata

      6 slices day-old bread
      4 ounces sharp process American
          cheese, shredded (1 cup)
   1½ cups diced, cooked chicken
      1 10½-ounce can condensed cream of
          chicken soup
      2 beaten eggs
      1 cup milk
      2 tablespoons finely chopped onion
      ¼ cup fine dry bread crumbs
      2 tablespoons butter or margarine,
          melted
      ¼ teaspoon paprika

Advance preparation: Trim crusts from bread slices; cut in half diagonally. Arrange *half* the bread triangles in bottom of an 8x8x2-inch baking dish. Sprinkle with shredded cheese. Top with chicken and remaining bread triangles. Combine soup and eggs; stir in milk and onion. Pour soup mixture over casserole. Cover; chill 6 to 24 hours.

   Before serving: Combine remaining ingredients. Sprinkle over casserole. Bake at 325° till set, about 1 hour. Let stand 10 minutes before serving. Makes 6 servings.

Tomato Salad Special

Cucumber and avocado pick up the flavor of the herb-seasoned marinade—

      1 medium cucumber
      2 ripe avocados
      1 cup salad oil
   ⅓ cup vinegar
      1 tablespoon lemon juice
      1 teaspoon sugar
      1 teaspoon dried basil, crushed
   ½ teaspoon dried marjoram, crushed
   ½ teaspoon salt
   ½ teaspoon dry mustard
   ⅛ teaspoon red pepper
      1 small clove garlic, crushed
      3 small tomatoes
      Lettuce

Advance preparation: Score cucumber lengthwise with fork; slice about ⅛ inch thick. Use melon baller to make balls from avocados. In screw-top jar combine salad oil, vinegar, lemon juice, sugar, crushed basil, crushed marjoram, salt, dry mustard, red pepper, and crushed garlic. Cover and shake. Pour over cucumber slices and avocado balls in bowl; marinate in refrigerator a few hours.

   Before serving: Cut each tomato into 6 wedges. Drain marinated vegetables, reserving dressing. Arrange cucumber slices, avocado balls, and tomato wedges on 6 lettuce-lined individual salad plates. Drizzle with reserved dressing. Makes 6 servings.

Elegant Fruit Medley

Has a touch of sherry—

      1 20½-ounce can pineapple tidbits
      1 16-ounce can peach slices, drained
      2 oranges, peeled and sectioned
   ¼ cup cream sherry
      Mint sprigs

Advance preparation: Drain pineapple, reserving syrup. Combine pineapple, peaches, and oranges. Combine reserved pineapple syrup and cream sherry; pour over fruit. Chill several hours. Garnish with mint. Serves 6.

STEAK DINNER (8)

Onion-Buttered Sirloin
Buttered Asparagus Spears
Fettuccine Alfredo
Cran-Raspberry Sherbet Mold
Vegetable Relishes
Buttermint Chiffon Pie
Coffee   Iced Tea

Want to serve steak in a different and easy-to-prepare way? Then, try delectable Onion-Buttered Sirloin. While the steak is broiling, simply brush on the butter mixture.

Such a delicious steak needs equally impressive accompaniments and Fettuccine Alfredo fits the bill. If you have a chafing dish, this is the time to bring it to the table. Cook the fettuccine and combine the butter, cream, and cheese. Then, bring the ingredients to the table and quickly assemble the Fettuccine Alfredo while your guests watch.

Fettuccine Alfredo

½ cup butter or margarine, softened
¼ cup whipping cream (room temperature)
½ cup grated Parmesan cheese
16 ounces fettuccine (medium noodles)
1 6-ounce can whole mushrooms, drained (about 1 cup)

In small mixer bowl cream butter or margarine. Beat in whipping cream, a little at a time, till mixture is well combined. Beat in Parmesan cheese. Set aside while cooking fettuccine in boiling, salted water for 10 to 12 minutes; stir pasta occasionally. Drain. Transfer pasta to warm chafing dish or serving bowl. Add the creamed mixture and toss till all fettuccine is well coated. Season with a little salt and freshly ground pepper. Stir in whole mushrooms. Serve at once with additional Parmesan cheese, if desired. Makes 8 servings.

Buttermint Chiffon Pie

Garnish with dollops of whipped cream—

1½ cups crushed chocolate wafers
½ cup sifted confectioners' sugar
6 tablespoons butter or margarine, melted
• • •
24 buttermints, crushed (½ cup)
1 envelope unflavored gelatin
1¼ cups milk
3 beaten egg yolks
Green food coloring
½ cup whipping cream
3 egg whites
¼ cup granulated sugar

Combine wafer crumbs, confectioners' sugar, and melted butter or margarine. Press into 9-inch pie plate; chill. In saucepan combine crushed mints and unflavored gelatin; gradually stir in milk and egg yolks. Cook and stir over medium-low heat till slightly thickened, 10 to 12 minutes. Stir in a few drops green food coloring; cool. Whip cream till soft peaks form. Beat egg whites till soft peaks form; gradually add granulated sugar, beating to stiff peaks. Fold egg yolk mixture, then whipped cream into egg whites. Spoon into pie shell; chill till firm, about 5 hours. Garnish with additional whipped cream.

To prevent a steak from curling while it is being broiled, slash through the fat edges, but not into the meat, at 1-inch intervals.

Onion-Buttered Sirloin

A man-pleasing main dish —

In small saucepan combine ½ cup butter or
margarine, ¼ cup snipped parsley, ¼ cup
minced onion, 2 teaspoons Worcestershire
sauce, ½ teaspoon dry mustard, and ½ teaspoon freshly ground pepper; heat together
till butter melts. Slash fat edges of a 4-pound
bone-in beef sirloin steak (about 1½ inches
thick) at 1-inch intervals; place steak on rack in
broiler pan. Broil 3 to 4 inches from heat for 10
to 12 minutes on each side for rare or 14 to 16
minutes on each side for medium, brushing
frequently with butter mixture. Serves 8.

Cran-Raspberry Sherbet Mold

    2 3-ounce packages raspberry-flavored
       gelatin
1½ cups boiling water
    1 pint raspberry sherbet
    1 tablespoon lemon juice
    1 16-ounce can whole cranberry sauce
      Lettuce

Dissolve gelatin in boiling water; stir in sherbet
and lemon juice. Chill, if necessary, till mixture
mounds. Mash cranberry sauce slightly with
fork; fold into gelatin mixture. Turn into
5-cup ring mold; chill till firm. Unmold on
lettuce-lined plate. Makes 8 servings.

Small pieces of onion and parsley in a well-
seasoned butter mixture add a distinctive
flavor to *Onion-Buttered Sirloin*. Serve this
juicy steak with buttered asparagus spears.

FRENCH DINNER (6)

Radishes with Salt
Mushroom-Sauced Tournedos
Tiny Whole Potatoes
Hard Rolls   Butter
Tossed Greens   French Dressing
Petits Pois
Pots de Crème
Burgundy   Coffee

Want to give a continental touch to a company meal? Then serve a French-inspired dinner. This exquisite meal of steak (tournedos), potatoes, salad, tiny peas (Petits Pois), and creamy chocolate dessert (Pots de Crème) is sure to delight your dinner guests.

To create the mood for this special occasion, decorate the table with a tiny Eiffel Tower centerpiece or miniature French tri-color flags (broad vertical stripes of blue, white, and red). And for an elegant touch, provide each guest with a hand-printed menu.

Mushroom-Sauced Tournedos

6 6-ounce beef tenderloin steaks,
1 inch thick
2 4½-ounce jars whole mushrooms,
drained
2 tablespoons butter
• • •
⅓ cup Burgundy
½ cup whipping cream

Trim excess fat from meat. In skillet saute whole mushrooms in butter; push to one side. Cook steaks in same skillet over medium heat for about 10 minutes (rare), turning once; remove meat to warm platter. Season with salt and pepper. Add wine to skillet; stir to loosen crusty bits from skillet. Add cream; cook and stir over low heat till slightly thickened, about 4 minutes. Serve mushroom sauce over steaks. Makes 6 servings.

Petits Pois

The name means small, green peas—

2 tablespoons chopped green onion
with tops
⅓ cup butter or margarine
1 cup chopped Boston lettuce
2 tablespoons snipped parsley
½ teaspoon sugar
¼ teaspoon salt
2 16-ounce cans tiny peas, drained

In saucepan cook onion in butter till tender but not brown. Add lettuce, parsley, sugar, salt, and dash pepper; cook till lettuce is wilted. Stir in peas; heat through. Serves 6.

French Dressing

½ cup salad oil
2 tablespoons vinegar
2 tablespoons lemon juice
1 teaspoon sugar
½ teaspoon salt
½ teaspoon paprika
½ teaspoon dry mustard
Dash cayenne

Combine all ingredients in screw-top jar; cover and shake well. Makes about ¾ cup.

Pots de Crème

Rich with chocolate and cream—

1 6-ounce package semisweet
chocolate pieces
1¼ cups light cream
2 egg yolks
Dash salt

In heavy saucepan combine chocolate and cream. Stir over low heat till blended and satin-smooth. Mixture should be *slightly thick but not boiling.* Beat egg yolks and salt till airy and thick. Gradually stir in hot chocolate mixture. Spoon into 6 pot de crème cups or small sherbets. Cover; chill till of pudding consistency, about 3 hours. Makes 6 servings.

Take advantage of the oriental quick-cooking technique by featuring Chicken-Steak Almond at your next dinner party. Have the ingredients ready on a tray, and then cook this delicious main dish at the table in a wok or an electric skillet. Round out the meal with the suggested oriental accompaniments.

Mandarin Meringues

2 egg whites
¼ teaspoon cream of tartar
½ cup sugar
2 11-ounce cans mandarin orange sections
1 tablespoon sugar
1½ teaspoons cornstarch
1 tablespoon lemon juice
¼ teaspoon ground ginger

Have whites at room temperature. Beat whites and cream of tartar to soft peaks. Gradually add ½ cup sugar, beating till very stiff peaks form and sugar is dissolved. Cover baking sheet with brown paper. Draw 4 circles on paper, each about 4 inches in diameter. Spread each with meringue, shaping into shells with back of spoon. Bake at 275° for 1 hour. Turn off heat; let shells dry in oven with door closed for 1 to 2 hours. Set aside.

Drain mandarin oranges, reserving ½ cup syrup. Combine 1 tablespoon sugar and cornstarch; stir in reserved syrup. Cook and stir till thickened. Stir in oranges, lemon juice, and ginger. Spoon orange mixture into meringue shells. Chill. Makes 4 servings.

Chicken-Steak Almond

As shown on page 6—

1 whole chicken breast, skinned and boned
8 to 10 ounces boneless beef sirloin steak
2 stalks celery
4 green onions
1 5- or 8½-ounce can water chestnuts, drained
2 tablespoons salad oil
1 6-ounce package frozen pea pods, thawed
3 cups chicken broth
3 tablespoons soy sauce
⅓ cup cornstarch
½ cup cold water
½ cup toasted slivered almonds

Cut chicken and sirloin steak into thin strips. Bias-slice the celery, green onions, and water chestnuts. Arrange meat, vegetables, and remaining ingredients on a serving tray.

In wok or electric skillet, quickly cook and stir meats and onion in hot oil. Add pea pods, celery, water chestnuts, chicken broth, and soy. Bring to boiling; cover and cook 2 to 3 minutes. Blend together cornstarch and water; add to chicken mixture. Cook and stir till thickened. Top with nuts; serve with chow mein noodles. Makes 4 servings.

Cucumber-Radish Plate

1 large cucumber, thinly sliced (1½ cups)
¾ cup sliced radish
½ cup vinegar
¼ cup sugar
¼ cup water
2 teaspoons finely snipped candied ginger
¼ teaspoon salt

In deep mixing bowl combine cucumber, radish, vinegar, sugar, water, ginger, and salt; cover and refrigerate for 2 to 4 hours. To serve, drain off marinade liquid; arrange vegetables on serving plate. Makes 4 servings.

```
┌─────────────────────────────────┐
│      SEMIFORMAL DINNER (8)        │
│                                   │
│      Consommé Madrilene           │
│   Pompano with Lemon Butter       │
│          White Wine               │
│   Cherry-Almond Glazed Pork       │
│  Baked Potatoes    Buttered Peas  │
│      Hot Rolls     Butter         │
│   Tossed Salad with Croutons      │
│        Coffee Angel Pie           │
│             Coffee                │
└─────────────────────────────────┘
```

Bring the elegance of a stately dinner to your dining table with this meal served in six separate courses—1. soup, 2. fish, 3. entrée (meat, vegetables, and rolls), 4. salad, 5. dessert, and 6. coffee. Surprisingly, this dinner is designed to be prepared and served without the added expense of hiring extra help.

Planning and prepreparation are the keys to making the dinner go smoothly. So, as soon as possible, plan the table setting, shopping list, and preparation schedule.

This occasion calls for your best linens, china, crystal, and silver. Aside from the basic place setting used for the entrée—dinner and bread-and-butter plates, glassware, knife, fork, and spoon, this meal requires some extras. You'll need soup dishes and spoons, plates to put under the soup dishes, plates for the fish, salad plates and forks, dessert plates and forks, and cups and saucers.

When setting up your preparation schedule, plan to do as much food preparation in advance as possible. Also, set the table for the first course and assemble dishes for other courses several hours ahead.

Serving this dinner requires careful organization since you have only the food and dishes for one course on the table at a time. Serve all the courses except the entrée and the coffee from the kitchen. Have the host carve the pork roast at the table, if desired. Then the meat, vegetables, and rolls are passed. Pour the coffee course at your place at the table. Refill wine glasses throughout the meal as needed.

Cherry-Almond Glazed Pork

  1 3-pound boneless pork loin roast
    Salt and pepper
  1 12-ounce jar cherry preserves
  ¼ cup red wine vinegar
  2 tablespoons light corn syrup
  ¼ teaspoon *each* ground cinnamon,
    ground nutmeg, and ground cloves
  ¼ cup slivered almonds, toasted

Rub roast with a little salt and pepper. Place on rack in shallow roasting pan. Roast, uncovered, at 325° for 2 to 2½ hours. Meanwhile, combine preserves, vinegar, syrup, spices, and ¼ teaspoon salt. Heat and stir till boiling; reduce heat and simmer 2 minutes. Add almonds. Keep sauce warm. Spoon some sauce over roast to glaze. Return to oven till meat thermometer reads 170°, about 30 minutes, basting with sauce several times. Pass remaining sauce with roast. Makes 8 servings.

Coffee Angel Pie

  2 egg whites
  ½ teaspoon vanilla
  ¼ teaspoon cream of tartar
  ½ cup sugar
  ½ cup finely chopped pecans
  1 pint coffee ice cream
  1 pint vanilla ice cream
    Caramel-Raisin Sauce

Beat together first 3 ingredients and ¼ teaspoon salt till soft peaks form. Gradually beat in sugar till very stiff peaks form and sugar is dissolved. Fold in nuts. Spread in well-buttered 9-inch pie plate, building up sides to form shell. Bake at 275° for 1 hour. Turn off heat; let dry in oven (door closed) for 1 hour. Cool. Pile scoops of ice cream in shell; freeze. Let stand 20 minutes at room temperature before serving. Serve with warm Caramel-Raisin Sauce. Serves 8.

Caramel-Raisin Sauce: Melt 3 tablespoons butter; stir in 1 cup brown sugar, one 6-ounce can evaporated milk, and dash salt. Cook and stir just till boiling. Remove from heat; add ½ cup light raisins and 1 teaspoon vanilla. Cool the mixture slightly.

Enhance the elegant tone of this meal by serving *Cherry-Almond Glazed Pork* on a large silver platter. Accompany the roast pork with the extra cherry-almond glaze.

Consommé Madrilene

    2 envelopes unflavored gelatin
    2 cups tomato juice
    4 beef bouillon cubes
    ¼ cup dry sherry
      Dash white pepper
      Snipped chives

Soften gelatin in *1 cup* juice. Heat and stir 2½ cups water and bouillon cubes till boiling. Add gelatin, stirring till dissolved; remove from heat. Add remaining juice, sherry, and pepper. Chill till partially set, stirring a few times. Chill till almost firm. Spoon into dishes; top with chives. Makes 8 servings.

Pompano with Lemon Butter

    2 pounds fresh or frozen pompano
      or sole fillets
    1 small onion, quartered
    6 tablespoons butter
    2 tablespoons lemon juice
    2 tablespoons snipped parsley

Thaw frozen fish. Cut fish into 8 portions. Place in greased 10-inch skillet. Add boiling water to cover. Add onion and 2 teaspoons salt. Simmer, covered, till fish flakes easily, about 5 minutes. Carefully remove fish. Melt butter; add lemon juice, parsley, and dash pepper. Serve with fish. Serves 8.

```
┌─────────────────────────────┐
│                             │
│    FONDUE SUPPER (6)        │
│                             │
│   Crispy Chicken Fondue     │
│     French Onion Pie        │
│        Fruit Salad          │
│     Brandied Chocolate      │
│                             │
└─────────────────────────────┘
```

"Fondue is fun" is a popular saying, and it's true for both the hostess (because it is easy to prepare) and the guests (because they are able to participate). If possible, use two fondue pots so everybody can reach one easily.

To avoid last-minute rush, prepare a salad, the fondue sauce, and the chicken early in the day; then chill. About 1½ hours before the meal, finish the preparation. First, set out the chicken and start the pie. Second, set the table and measure the ingredients for the dessert hot chocolate. Let your guests enjoy fonduing the chicken at the table.

Crispy Chicken Fondue

½ cup catsup
¼ cup molasses
2 tablespoons lemon juice
½ teaspoon ground ginger
¼ teaspoon pepper
4 large chicken breasts, skinned, boned, and cut in strips
¾ cup fine saltine cracker crumbs
Salad oil

For sauce combine catsup, molasses, lemon juice, ½ teaspoon salt, ginger, and pepper; chill. Coat chicken strips with cracker crumbs. Loosely thread each strip onto bamboo skewer in accordion fashion; chill. To serve, have skewered chicken strips at room temperature on serving plate. Pour oil into fondue cooker to no more than ½ capacity or to depth of 2 inches. Heat over range to 400°. Add 1 teaspoon salt. Transfer cooker to fondue burner. Fry chicken in hot oil for 2 to 3 minutes. Cool slightly; dip in sauce. Serves 6.

French Onion Pie

1 *unbaked* 9-inch pastry shell (see page 23)
1 3½-ounce can French-fried onions (2 cups)
4 eggs
2 cups milk
2 ounces sharp process American cheese, shredded (½ cup)
½ teaspoon salt
Dash cayenne
4 ounces sharp process American cheese, shredded (1 cup)

Bake pastry shell at 450° till golden, about 7 to 8 minutes. Reduce oven temperature to 325°. While pastry is still warm, fill bottom with *1½ cups* of the French-fried onions. Beat eggs slightly; blend in milk, the ½ cup shredded American cheese, the salt, and cayenne. Pour over French-fried onions in pastry shell. Sprinkle the 1 cup shredded American cheese over pie. Bake at 325° for 45 minutes. Sprinkle remaining onions around edge of pie. Bake till knife inserted just off-center comes out clean, about 5 to 10 minutes more. Let stand at room temperature 10 minutes before serving. Makes 6 servings.

Brandied Chocolate

1 1-ounce square unsweetened chocolate, cut up
3 tablespoons sugar
2 teaspoons instant coffee powder
Dash salt
½ cup water
2 cups light cream
1 cup milk
⅓ cup brandy
½ cup whipping cream

In saucepan combine cut-up chocolate, sugar, coffee powder, salt, and water. Cook and stir over low heat till chocolate melts. Bring to boiling, stirring constantly; let simmer 2 minutes. Gradually stir in light cream and milk. Heat just to boiling. Stir in brandy. Pour into hot cups or mugs. Whip whipping cream; spoon some atop each mug. Serves 6.

Serve generous wedges of *French Onion Pie* as an accompaniment to *Crispy Chicken Fondue*. This quiche-like dish, rich with cheese and eggs, is also delicious with beef fondue.

```
┌──────────────────────────────┐
│     VEGETARIAN SUPPER (6)     │
│                              │
│  Vegetable and Soy Macaroni Soup │
│  Pumpkin Seed Whole Wheat Bread  │
│        Spinach Salad         │
│   Fresh Fruit  or  Baked Apples  │
│     Tea    Lemon    Honey    │
└──────────────────────────────┘
```

Searching for an unusual party theme? Then treat your guests to an up-to-the-minute vegetarian supper. Serve tasty Vegetable and Soy Macaroni Soup, mouth-watering Pumpkin Seed Whole Wheat Bread, tangy Spinach Salad, and a dessert of fresh fruits or baked apples sweetened with honey. Accompany with a beverage of tea, plus lemon and honey.

Most of the ingredients in the recipes are available at your local supermarket. For the few specialty items called for, check with your local health food stores.

Vegetable and Soy Macaroni Soup

A hearty, meatless main dish—

    1 cup lentils
         • • •
    5 cups water
    4 vegetable bouillon cubes
    1 28-ounce can tomatoes, cut up
    2 cups shredded cabbage
    ¾ cup chopped onion
    ½ cup chopped carrot
    1 clove garlic, minced
         • • •
    1 cup uncooked soy macaroni
    Salt

Rinse lentils; drain and place in soup kettle. Add water, bouillon cubes, undrained tomatoes, cabbage, onion, carrot, and garlic. Cover and simmer about 1 hour. Add uncooked soy macaroni. Cook, covered, until vegetables and macaroni are done, about 20 minutes. Season to taste with salt. Makes 6 servings.

Pumpkin Seed Whole Wheat Bread

Next time, substitute sunflower seeds —

    2 packages active dry yeast
    5 cups whole wheat flour
 2⅓ cups milk
    1 tablespoon salt
    2 tablespoons salad oil
    ½ cup honey
    1 cup hulled pumpkin seeds, coarsely
       chopped

In large mixer bowl combine yeast and *2 cups* whole wheat flour. Heat milk, salt, salad oil, and honey just till warm, stirring occasionally to blend in honey. Add to dry mixture in mixer bowl. Beat at low speed of electric mixer for ½ minute, scraping bowl constantly. Beat 3 minutes at high speed. By hand, stir in pumpkin seeds and enough remaining flour to make a soft dough. Turn out on lightly floured surface and knead till smooth and elastic, about 10 minutes.

Place in greased bowl, turning once to grease surface. Cover and let rise in warm place till double, about 2 hours. Punch down dough and shape into two loaves. Place in two greased 8½x4½x2⅝-inch loaf pans. Cover and let rise until almost double, about 1¼ hours. Bake at 375° about 45 minutes. (If crust browns too quickly, cover bread loosely with foil last 15 minutes.) Remove; cool. Makes 2.

Spinach Salad

    1 pound fresh spinach
    ½ small head lettuce
    1 green onion and top, sliced
    ⅓ cup olive oil
    3 tablespoons lemon juice
    1 tablespoon honey
    1 tablespoon toasted sesame seed

Wash spinach and pat dry with paper toweling. Tear spinach into a salad bowl. Tear lettuce into bite-sized pieces. Toss spinach and lettuce with onion. Combine olive oil, lemon juice, and honey. Just before serving, add dressing to salad and toss to coat. Sprinkle sesame seed atop. Makes 6 servings.

```
┌─────────────────────────────┐
│    SEAFOOD SUPPER (8)        │
│                             │
│  Baked Shrimp and Crab Combo │
│ Dilled Tomatoes  Artichoke Hearts │
│    Rolls     Butter Balls    │
│      Apricot Parfaits        │
│       Coffee    Tea          │
└─────────────────────────────┘
```

Baked Shrimp and Crab Combo

For added charm, serve this in baking shells—

2 10½-ounce cans condensed cream
  of celery soup
½ cup milk
2 beaten eggs
¼ cup grated Parmesan cheese
2 7½-ounce cans crab meat, drained,
  flaked, and cartilage removed
2 4½-ounce cans shrimp, drained
1 6-ounce can sliced mushrooms,
  drained
⅓ cup fine dry bread crumbs
¼ cup grated Parmesan cheese
2 tablespoons butter or margarine,
  melted

Combine cream of celery soup, milk, eggs, and ¼ cup Parmesan cheese in a saucepan. Stir over low heat till cheese is melted and mixture is hot. Stir in crab, shrimp, and mushrooms. Spoon mixture into 8 large baking shells or individual casseroles.

Toss bread crumbs with ¼ cup Parmesan cheese and the melted butter. Sprinkle crumbs over seafood mixture. Bake at 375° till mixture is hot and crumbs are browned, about 20 minutes. Garnish with parsley and twists of lemon and lime, if desired. Makes 8 servings.

Artichoke Hearts

Drain two 16-ounce cans artichoke hearts *or* cook and drain three 9-ounce packages frozen artichoke hearts. Put into a casserole and dot with butter. Cover and heat at 375° about 20 minutes. Sprinkle with snipped parsley and chopped canned pimiento. Serves 8.

Dilled Tomatoes

Remove stems from 4 large tomatoes; cut in half crosswise with sawtooth cut. (Or cut tops off of 8 small tomatoes.) Arrange tomato halves in baking dish, cut sides up. Sprinkle with salt, pepper, and dried dillweed. Bake at 375° till heated through, about 20 minutes. Makes 8 servings.

This supper is easy on the cook since the main dish, tomatoes, and artichokes are all heated in the oven at the same time. Serving is also simplified because the seafood mixture is portioned in individual bakers.

Prepare the Butter Balls in advance and chill them until serving time. To make *Butter Balls,* cut firm (not too cold) butter sticks into ½-inch pats. Form into a ball with fingers. Scald two butter paddles in boiling water, then chill paddles in ice water. Put butter ball on scored side of paddle. Holding bottom paddle still, move top paddle in circular motion using light pressure. If butter clings to paddles, scald and chill paddles again.

Apricot Parfaits

Make these ahead of time and refrigerate—

1 30-ounce can unpeeled apricot halves
½ cup chopped pecans
½ cup toasted coconut
• • •
2 3- or 3¼-ounce packages *regular*
  vanilla pudding mix
¼ teaspoon almond extract
1½ cups dairy sour cream

Drain apricots. Puree fruit and chill. Combine pecans and toasted coconut; set aside. Prepare vanilla pudding mix according to package directions. Add almond extract to cooked pudding. Chill 1 hour. Alternately layer pudding, pecan-coconut mixture, sour cream, and apricot purée in 8 parfait glasses. Chill till serving time. Makes 8 servings.

```
┌─────────────────────────────────┐
│                                 │
│      BARBECUE SUPPER (4)        │
│                                 │
│      Barbecued Spareribs        │
│   Potato Bake    Corn on the Cob│
│      Orange-Spinach Toss        │
│      Raspberry Shortcake        │
│        Beer    Frostea          │
│                                 │
└─────────────────────────────────┘
```

Everyone likes the special flavor of meat cooked over the coals, so get out the grill and have a barbecue. While hubby's watching the ribs, potatoes, and corn, you can put together the dessert and fix the salad and beverage. In short order, supper will be ready.

Frostea

> 2 tablespoons instant tea powder
> 3 cups ice water
> 6 tablespoons frozen pineapple
>   juice concentrate, thawed
> 1 pint pineapple sherbet

Dissolve tea in water; add pineapple concentrate. Pour into 4 tall glasses; add a scoop of sherbet to each. Stir slightly. Serves 4.

Orange-Spinach Toss

> 4 cups fresh spinach, torn in
>   bite-sized pieces
> 3 oranges, peeled and sectioned
> 4 slices bacon, crisp-cooked,
>   drained, and crumbled
> ½ cup chopped peanuts
>   • • •
> 1 envelope French salad dressing mix

In salad bowl combine torn spinach, orange sections, bacon, and peanuts. Prepare French salad dressing mix according to package directions. Pour desired amount of dressing over orange-spinach mixture, tossing lightly to mix. Makes 4 servings.

Raspberry Shortcake

A rich, flavorful dessert—

> 2 10-ounce packages frozen red
>   raspberries, thawed
> 1 tablespoon sugar
> 1 tablespoon cornstarch
> 1 teaspoon vanilla
>   • • •
> 1½ cups sifted all-purpose flour
> 2 tablespoons sugar
> 2 teaspoons baking powder
> ¼ teaspoon salt
> 6 tablespoons butter or margarine
> 1 beaten egg
> ⅓ cup light cream
> Whipped cream

Drain raspberries, reserving syrup. In small saucepan combine 1 tablespoon sugar and cornstarch; blend in reserved syrup. Cook and stir till thickened and bubbly; cook 1 minute more. Cool slightly; stir in raspberries and vanilla. Chill thoroughly.

Sift together flour, 2 tablespoons sugar, baking powder, and salt; cut in butter till mixture resembles coarse crumbs. Combine egg and light cream; add all at once, stirring just to moisten. Turn dough onto lightly floured surface; knead gently for ½ minute. Pat or roll to ½-inch thickness. Cut 4 biscuits with floured 2½-inch cutter. Bake on ungreased baking sheet at 450° till golden brown, about 10 minutes. Split biscuits; fill and top with raspberry sauce. Top with dollops of whipped cream. Makes 4 servings.

Corn on the Cob

Grill alongside the meat—

Remove husks from fresh corn. Remove silk with a stiff brush. Place each ear on a sheet of foil. Spread corn liberally with softened butter; sprinkle with salt and pepper.

Wrap foil securely around each ear of corn—fold or twist foil around ends. Place on grill and roast over hot coals till corn is tender, about 15 to 20 minutes; turn ears frequently. Pass extra butter, salt, and pepper.

Summer is barbecue time, and what could be more delicious than *Barbecued Spareribs,* *Potato Bake,* and *Corn on the Cob?* Accompany this man-pleasing supper with mugs of beer.

Barbecued Spareribs

   1 8-ounce can tomato sauce with
       chopped onion
 ⅓ cup brown sugar
 ⅓ cup bottled steak sauce
 ⅓ cup salad oil
 ¼ cup vinegar
 ¼ teaspoon salt
  4 pounds spareribs

Combine all ingredients except spareribs; set aside. Season ribs with a little additional salt. Place, bone side down, on grill over slow coals. Grill about 20 minutes; turn meaty side down and grill till browned. Turn meaty side up; grill 20 minutes more. Brush meaty side with barbecue sauce. Continue grilling, without turning, till meat is tender, 20 to 30 minutes more, basting occasionally with sauce mixture. Makes 4 servings.

Potato Bake

  2 large potatoes, peeled and sliced
      ⅛ inch thick (4 cups)
  1 large onion, sliced and separated
      into rings
       ● ● ●
  ¼ teaspoon seasoned salt
  ¼ teaspoon celery seed
  ¼ teaspoon garlic salt
    Dash pepper
  2 tablespoons butter or margarine

On large sheet of foil, layer ⅓ of the potatoes and onions. Combine seasonings; sprinkle ¼ teaspoon salt mixture over vegetables. Dot with some of the butter or margarine. Repeat, making two more layers. Seal foil with double fold. Bake at 350° till potatoes are tender, about 45 minutes, *or* grill over medium coals for 50 to 60 minutes. Serves 4.

Entertaining 10 to 16 Guests

As your guest list increases in size, choosing the right types of foods to serve becomes especially important. It is best to serve foods that are easy to prepare in larger quantities, such as casseroles, roasts, salads, tortes, and large cakes.

Remember, too, that you will need adequate seating space. Buffet-style or help-yourself service proves useful when your dining table doesn't expand enough to handle 10 or more people comfortably. Let guests balance plates or trays on their laps or provide seating space at several small tables.

And just because there are more guests doesn't mean that you have to eliminate guest participation. Instead, get your guests involved by planning a potluck or a make-it-yourself pizza party.

Set up several card tables to accommodate guests at a buffet. This buffet dinner for 12 features *Rib Roast with Onion Butter, Curried Rice,* buttered broccoli spears, fruit salad plate with *Orange Dressing,* and warm rolls.

RECIPES

(For appetizer and snack recipes see pages 98 to 103. Recipes particularly suited for medium groups include Caviar Log, Hot Cheese-Chive Dip, Stuffed Mushrooms, and Liverwurst Rolls.)

Deluxe Fruit Cup

Drain one 13½-ounce can pineapple tidbits, reserving 2 tablespoons syrup. Combine pineapple; one 10-ounce package frozen blueberries, thawed and well drained; 2 cups cantaloupe balls; and one 11-ounce can mandarin orange sections, well drained. Spoon into 12 sherbets. In small bowl combine 1 cup cranberry-orange relish and reserved pineapple syrup. Drizzle over fruits. Chill thoroughly. Makes 12 first-course servings.

Creamy Vegetable Soup

¾ cup chopped celery
½ cup chopped carrot
⅓ cup finely chopped onion
3½ cups chicken broth
½ cup sifted all-purpose flour
1 cup milk
½ cup light cream
½ cup butter or margarine

In saucepan cook celery, carrot, and onion in *2 cups* of the chicken broth till tender. Blend flour and remaining chicken broth; add to vegetables in saucepan. Cook and stir till thickened and bubbly. Add milk, cream, and butter; heat through—do not boil. Makes 10 to 12 first-course servings.

Zippy Tomato Refresher

Combine 6 cups tomato juice, two 10½-ounce cans condensed beef broth, 1 teaspoon Worcestershire sauce, dash bottled hot pepper sauce, and dash garlic powder. Chill. Makes 14 to 16 first-course servings.

Brunch Egg Casserole

Spread 4 cups toasted bread cubes (6 slices) in bottom of greased 13½x8¾x1¾-inch baking dish. Sprinkle 8 ounces natural Cheddar cheese, shredded (2 cups), over bread. Blend 8 slightly beaten eggs, 4 cups milk, 1 teaspoon salt, 1 teaspoon prepared mustard, ¼ teaspoon onion powder, and ⅛ teaspoon pepper. Pour over bread-cheese mixture. Bake at 325° till egg mixture is set, 40 to 45 minutes. Meanwhile, crisp-cook and crumble 10 slices bacon. Sprinkle atop casserole during last 10 minutes of baking. Makes 10 servings.

Salmon-Rice Bake

1 cup long grain rice
4 10½-ounce cans condensed cream of celery soup
¾ cup milk
3 16-ounce cans salmon, drained, boned, and broken into large pieces
3 10-ounce packages frozen mixed vegetables, cooked and drained
2 6-ounce cans sliced mushrooms, drained
3 tablespoons butter or margarine
2 cups soft bread crumbs

Cook rice according to package directions. Blend soup and milk; stir in rice, salmon, vegetables, and mushrooms. Turn into two 2-quart casseroles. Bake, covered, at 350° for 50 minutes. Melt butter; toss with bread crumbs. Sprinkle crumb mixture around edge of casseroles. Bake, uncovered, 10 minutes more. Makes 14 servings.

Twin casseroles

Next time the menu calls for a casserole, → keep the cost low but the appeal high by serving tasty *Salmon-Rice Bake.*

Sour Cream-Topped Ham Bake

2½ cups long grain rice
¼ cup butter or margarine
3 tablespoons French salad dressing
    mix
1 tablespoon instant minced onion
6 cups cubed fully cooked ham
1 6-ounce can sliced mushrooms,
    drained
2 10-ounce packages frozen peas,
    thawed
5 cups hot water
3 cups dairy sour cream

Brown the rice in butter or margarine. Remove from heat; stir in dressing mix, onion, ham, mushrooms, and *half* of the peas. Turn into two 8x8x2-inch baking dishes. Add *2½ cups* hot water to *each* baking dish. Cover with foil and bake at 350° for 60 to 70 minutes, stirring occasionally. Spread sour cream atop; place *half* of the remaining peas in the center of *each* baking dish. Bake 5 minutes more to heat sour cream and peas. Makes 16 servings.

Oyster-Corn Bread Stuffed Turkey

1 10-ounce package corn bread mix
10 cups fresh bread cubes (14 slices)
2 tablespoons instant minced onion
1 tablespoon rubbed sage
2 10-ounce cans frozen oysters,
    thawed
½ cup butter or margarine, melted
1 20-pound ready-to-cook turkey

Prepare corn bread mix according to package directions. Cool and crumble. Toss with bread cubes, onion, sage, 2 teaspoons salt, and ⅛ teaspoon pepper. Drain oysters, reserving ½ cup liquid. Chop oysters; add to bread mixture with reserved oyster liquid, melted butter, and ½ cup water. Toss well. Salt cavities of bird. Spoon stuffing into cavities; tie legs to tail. Place, breast side up, on rack in shallow roasting pan. Cap loosely with foil. Roast at 325° for 6 to 6½ hours. Uncover last 45 minutes; cut band of skin or string between legs and tail. Let stand 15 to 20 minutes before carving. Makes 16 to 18 servings.

Dilled Cheese Casserole

⅓ cup butter or margarine
½ cup sifted all-purpose flour
1 tablespoon prepared mustard
5 cups milk
10 ounces sharp process American
    cheese, shredded (2½ cups)
5 beaten egg yolks
1 7-ounce package macaroni,
    cooked and drained
2½ cups cream-style cottage
    cheese
1 cup finely chopped dill pickle
2 cups soft rye bread crumbs
2 tablespoons butter, melted

In large saucepan melt ⅓ cup butter; blend in flour, mustard, and 1¼ teaspoons salt. Add milk. Cook and stir till bubbly. Add shredded cheese; cook and stir till melted. Stir some hot mixture into egg yolks; return to hot mixture. Cook and stir till bubbly; stir in macaroni. Spread *one-fourth* of mixture in *each* of two 2-quart casseroles. Combine cottage cheese and pickle; spread atop macaroni layer. Top with remaining macaroni. Combine crumbs and melted butter; sprinkle atop. Bake at 350° about 30 minutes. Makes 12 servings.

After stuffing neck cavity, place turkey, neck down, in a large bowl. Then, spoon the oyster-corn bread stuffing into body cavity.

Chicken Oriental

Cut the recipe in half for 6 servings—

6 large chicken breasts, halved
½ cup sifted all-purpose flour
¼ cup salad oil
1½ cups coarsely chopped onion
1 cup sliced celery
1 clove garlic, minced
2 10½-ounce cans condensed cream
    of mushroom soup
½ cup dry sherry
2 tablespoons soy sauce
1 6-ounce can sliced mushrooms
1 8-ounce can water chestnuts
2 6-ounce packages frozen
    pea pods, thawed

Coat chicken with mixture of flour, 1 teaspoon salt, and dash pepper. In 5-quart Dutch oven brown 4 chicken pieces at a time in hot oil. Remove chicken. Cook onion, celery, and garlic in same oil just till tender. Blend in soup, sherry, and soy. Drain mushrooms and water chestnuts; thinly slice water chestnuts. Add to soup mixture; bring to boiling. Place chicken in sauce. Cover; simmer 30 minutes. Add pea pods. Cover; simmer till chicken is done, 10 minutes. Spoon some sauce over chicken; pass remainder. Makes 12 servings.

Saucy Pork Roast

Pineapple sauce complements pork flavor—

1 6-pound boneless pork loin roast
1 cup pineapple juice
1 8¾-ounce can crushed pineapple
½ cup dry sherry
½ cup light corn syrup
2 tablespoons soy sauce
1 teaspoon ground ginger
3 tablespoons cornstarch

Place meat on rack in shallow roasting pan. Roast at 325° till meat thermometer registers 170°, about 2¾ to 3 hours. Combine next 6 ingredients; stir into cornstarch in saucepan. Cook and stir till thickened and bubbly. Serve hot with roast. Makes 16 servings.

Fruit-Stuffed Pork Crown

1 7-pound crown roast of pork
    (about 18 ribs)
6 cups packaged stuffing mix
1 medium apple, chopped
½ cup raisins
2 teaspoons grated orange peel
1 small orange, peeled
1 cup chopped celery
¼ cup butter or margarine
1 16-ounce can whole cranberry sauce
2 tablespoons brown sugar
1 tablespoon instant minced onion

Place roast in shallow roasting pan, bones up. Season with salt and pepper. Wrap bone tips with foil. Insert meat thermometer in loin, making sure it doesn't touch bone. Roast, uncovered, at 325° for 2¼ hours.

Meanwhile, combine next 4 ingredients. Section orange, reserving juice. Add water to juice to make ½ to ¾ cup liquid. Add orange and liquid to stuffing; mix lightly. Cook celery in butter till tender. Add cranberries, brown sugar, onion, and ½ teaspoon salt; bring to boil. Pour over stuffing; toss to mix. Fill roast with stuffing; cover stuffing with foil. Place remaining stuffing in greased 1½-quart casserole; cover and bake alongside roast. Continue roasting till meat thermometer registers 170°, about 1 hour longer. Serves 12 to 14.

Ham Stroganoff

1⅓ cups chopped onion
¼ cup butter or margarine
1 tablespoon all-purpose flour
1 cup milk
6 cups cubed fully cooked ham
4 cups dairy sour cream
1 cup sliced ripe olives
¼ cup dry sherry
⅔ cup toasted slivered almonds
    Hot cooked noodles

Cook onion in butter till tender; stir in flour. Add milk. Cook and stir till thickened and bubbly. Stir in ham, sour cream, olives, sherry, and almonds; heat but do not boil. Serve over noodles. Makes 12 servings.

Having an extra-special dinner party? Then choose *Beef Wellington* as the entrée. Cover a beef tenderloin with liver pâté and a flaky pasty casing for this elegant dish.

Beef Brisket in Beer

    1 4-pound beef brisket, trimmed of fat
    1 onion, sliced
    ¼ cup chili sauce
    2 tablespoons brown sugar
    1 clove garlic, minced
    1 12-ounce can beer (1½ cups)
    2 tablespoons all-purpose flour

Season meat with salt and pepper. Place in 13x9x2-inch baking pan; cover with onion. Combine next 4 ingredients; pour over meat. Cover with foil. Bake at 350° for 3½ hours. Uncover; bake 30 minutes, basting occasionally with juices. Skim fat from drippings; measure liquid and add water to make 1 cup. Blend flour and ½ cup cold water; combine with drippings. Cook and stir till bubbly; pass with meat. Cut meat across grain. Serves 10.

Leg of Lamb Mediterranean

Combine 4 teaspoons salt, 2 teaspoons pepper, and 2 teaspoons dried oregano, crushed; rub into one 8-pound leg of lamb. Roast lamb on rack in shallow roasting pan at 325° for 3 hours. Remove meat and rack from pan; set aside. Drain excess fat from pan juices. Place roast in pan without rack. Arrange 1 small lemon, sliced, atop lamb; secure with wooden picks. Surround roast with three 9-ounce packages frozen artichoke hearts, thawed. Combine two 8-ounce cans tomato sauce, 2 cups water, and 2 cloves garlic, minced; pour over roast. Continue roasting till meat thermometer reads 175° to 180°, about 45 minutes more. Baste occasionally with sauce. Place roast on platter; remove wooden picks. Accompany roast with artichoke sauce served over hot cooked rice. Serves 12 to 14.

Beef Wellington

Place 4-pound beef tenderloin on rack in shallow baking pan. Roast at 425° till meat thermometer reads 130°, about 45 minutes. Reserve drippings. Cool meat. Sift 2 cups sifted all-purpose flour and ½ teaspoon salt; cut in ⅔ cup shortening till mixture resembles coarse crumbs. Slowly add ⅓ to ½ cup cold water, tossing with fork till dampened. Form ball. Roll to 14x12-inch rectangle; spread two 2¾-ounce cans liver pâté to within ½ inch of edges. Center meat, top down, on pastry. Draw up long sides; overlap. Brush with 1 beaten egg; seal. Trim ends; fold up. Brush with egg; seal. Place on greased baking sheet, seam down. Add pastry cutouts. Brush with egg. Bake at 425° about 35 minutes.

For gravy combine reserved drippings, 1½ cups water, and 2 beef bouillon cubes in saucepan. Heat and stir till bouillon dissolves. Blend ¼ cup all-purpose flour and ½ cup cold water; add to pan with ½ teaspoon dried basil, crushed, and ⅓ cup Burgundy. Cook and stir till bubbly. Season with salt and pepper. Serve with roast. Serves 12 to 14.

Mexicali Meat Ring

> 3 beaten eggs
> Spicy Sauce
> 2 cups soft bread crumbs
> ½ cup crushed corn chips
> 1 tablespoon snipped parsley
> 3 pounds ground beef
> Hot cooked noodles

In large bowl combine eggs, *1 cup* cooled Spicy Sauce, crumbs, corn chips, parsley, and 1 teaspoon salt. Add beef; mix well. Press into 6-cup ring mold. Unmold on shallow baking pan. Bake at 350° for 1¼ hours. Carefully transfer to platter. Serve with noodles and *warmed* Spicy Sauce. Serves 12.

Spicy Sauce: Cook ¾ cup chopped onion and 1 clove garlic, minced, in 3 tablespoons salad oil till tender. Add two 16-ounce cans tomatoes, cut up; two 6-ounce cans tomato paste; 1 teaspoon *each* salt, sugar, and chili powder; ½ teaspoon pepper; and 1 bay leaf. Simmer, uncovered, 30 minutes. Remove leaf.

Oriental Steak Skillet

> 5 pounds beef round steak, ½ inch thick
> 1½ cups sifted all-purpose flour
> ¾ cup shortening
> 3 10½-ounce cans condensed beef broth
> 1 large onion, cut in thin wedges
> 1 teaspoon ground ginger
> 2 8-ounce cans water chestnuts
> 3 green peppers, cut in strips
> ⅔ cup soy sauce
> 6 tomatoes, cut in wedges
> Hot cooked rice

Cut steak in ¼-inch wide strips. Combine *1 cup* flour and ½ teaspoon pepper; use to coat meat, coating ⅙ of the meat at a time. Using a 6-quart Dutch oven *and* a 10-inch skillet, brown the meat in portions in hot shortening. When browning is completed, place all meat in Dutch oven. Add broth, 2 cups water, onion, and ginger. Cover; cook till meat is tender, 45 minutes. Drain and slice water chestnuts; add to meat with green pepper. Heat through. Blend remaining flour and soy. Add to meat; cook and stir till bubbly. Stir in tomatoes. Heat. Serve over hot cooked rice. Serves 16.

Beef with Yorkshire Pudding

> 1 8-pound beef standing rib roast
> 4 eggs
> 2 cups milk
> 2 cups sifted all-purpose flour

Place roast, fat side up, in shallow roasting pan. Season with salt and pepper. Roast, uncovered, at 325° till meat thermometer registers 140° for rare, 160° for medium, and 170° for well-done. Allow about 3¼ hours for rare, about 4 hours for medium, and about 4¾ hours for well-done. Remove meat from pan. Cover; keep warm. Reserve ¼ cup meat drippings. Increase oven to 400°. Combine eggs, milk, flour, and 1 teaspoon salt. Beat 1½ minutes with rotary beater or electric mixer. Pour *half* the reserved drippings into *each* of two 9x9x2-inch baking pans. Pour *half* the batter into each pan. Bake at 400° for 30 minutes. Serve with roast. Makes 12 servings.

Add a cooling touch to the meal by serving *Frosty Fruit Cubes,* an appetizing frozen salad that uses instant pudding for its base.

Frosty Fruit Cubes

 1 3⅝- or 3¾-ounce package *instant* vanilla pudding mix
 2 cups frozen dessert topping, thawed
 ½ cup mayonnaise or salad dressing
 2 tablespoons lemon juice
   • • •
 2 large bananas
 1 13½-ounce can crushed pineapple, drained
 ⅓ cup slivered almonds, toasted
  Lettuce

Prepare pudding mix according to package directions. Stir in dessert topping, mayonnaise, and lemon juice. Dice bananas. Combine bananas, pineapple, and almonds. Fold into pudding mixture. Turn into 11x7x1½-inch baking pan; freeze till firm. Remove from freezer and let stand 10 minutes. Cut into 1-inch cubes; serve on lettuce. If desired, top with additional slivered almonds. Makes 12 servings.

Frozen Fruit Loaf

Spiced peaches add extra flavor —

 1 8-ounce package cream cheese, softened
 ⅓ cup mayonnaise or salad dressing
 ¼ cup sugar
 1 cup whipping cream
 1 16-ounce can pitted dark sweet cherries, well drained and halved
 1 17-ounce can spiced whole peaches, drained and chopped
 1 13½-ounce can pineapple tidbits, drained
  Red food coloring

Beat cream cheese till fluffy; beat in mayonnaise and sugar. Whip cream; fold into cream cheese mixture. Gently fold in cherries, peaches, and pineapple. Tint pink with food coloring. Pour into 9x5x3-inch loaf pan. Freeze till firm, about 6 hours or overnight. Let stand at room temperature about 25 minutes before slicing. Makes 14 to 16 servings.

Creamy Asparagus Salad

An elegant molded vegetable salad —

 2 10-ounce cans cut asparagus spears
 3 envelopes unflavored gelatin
 4 chicken bouillon cubes
 1 tablespoon instant minced onion
 2 teaspoons sugar
   • • •
 2 cups dairy sour cream
 1 cup mayonnaise or salad dressing
 ¼ cup chopped canned pimiento
 2 tablespoons snipped parsley
 2 tablespoons lemon juice

Drain asparagus, reserving liquid. Add water to reserved liquid to make 2½ cups. Soften gelatin in the liquid. Add bouillon cubes, onion, and sugar. Heat to dissolve gelatin and bouillon cubes. Chill till partially set. Stir in sour cream, mayonnaise or salad dressing, pimiento, parsley, lemon juice, and asparagus. Spoon into 11¾x7½x1¾-inch baking dish. Chill till firm. Makes 12 servings.

Vegetable-Crouton Toss

    2 16-ounce cans cut green beans,
        drained
    1 16-ounce can sliced carrots,
        drained
    1 16-ounce can peas, drained
    1 16-ounce can whole kernel corn,
        drained
    ½ medium onion, thinly sliced and
        separated into rings
            • • •
    ½ cup vinegar
    ⅓ cup sugar
    ¼ cup salad oil
    1 teaspoon salt
    ½ teaspoon dried basil, crushed
    ⅛ teaspoon pepper
            • • •
    Parmesan Croutons

Combine beans, carrots, peas, corn, and onion in large salad bowl. In screw-top jar combine vinegar, sugar, oil, salt, basil, and pepper. Cover and shake vigorously. Pour over vegetables, tossing lightly. Refrigerate several hours or overnight, stirring occasionally. Drain. Toss with Parmesan Croutons. Serves 16.

Parmesan Croutons: In large skillet melt 2 tablespoons butter or margarine; stir in 1 teaspoon onion salt. Add 2 cups bite-sized toasted corn or rice cereal and ¼ cup grated Parmesan cheese. Heat and stir till coated, 5 minutes. Spread on paper toweling to cool.

Yogurt-Fruit Combo

    2 8-ounce cartons orange yogurt
        (2 cups)
    ⅓ cup mayonnaise or salad dressing
    1 11-ounce can mandarin orange
        sections, drained
    1 20-ounce can pineapple tidbits,
        drained
    1 16-ounce can pitted light sweet
        cherries, drained and halved
    1 cup miniature marshmallows

Stir together yogurt and mayonnaise. Fold in fruits and marshmallows. Chill at least 1 hour before serving. Makes 10 to 12 servings.

Berry-Apricot Mold

    1 8¾-ounce can unpeeled apricot
        halves (1 cup)
    2 3-ounce packages or 1 6-ounce
        package lemon-flavored gelatin
    1 12-ounce can apricot nectar, chilled
        (1½ cups)
    1½ cups sliced strawberries
    ¼ cup dairy sour cream
    ¼ cup mayonnaise or salad dressing
    Grated lemon peel

Drain and coarsely chop apricots, reserving syrup. Add water to syrup to equal 2 cups liquid. Pour into saucepan and bring to boiling. Add gelatin and stir till dissolved. Remove from heat. Stir in chilled apricot nectar. Chill till partially set. Fold in chopped apricots and strawberries. Turn into 5½- or 6½-cup ring mold; chill till firm. Unmold onto serving plate. Stir together sour cream, mayonnaise, and a little grated lemon peel; serve with salad. Makes 10 servings.

Tangy Cauliflower Salad

Cut the recipe in half to make 6 servings—

    2 medium heads cauliflower, separated
        into cauliflowerets (about 8 cups)
    4 medium carrots, cut in 2-inch julienne
        strips (2 cups)
    ⅔ cup French salad dressing
    1 tablespoon lemon juice
    ¼ teaspoon dried basil, crushed
    2 ounces blue cheese, crumbled
        (½ cup)
    Lettuce
    2 small avocados, peeled and sliced

Cut cauliflowerets in half lengthwise. In large saucepan cook cauliflower and carrots in boiling, salted water till tender, 8 to 10 minutes. Drain well. Season with salt and pepper. Combine French dressing, lemon juice, and basil; toss with cauliflower, carrots, and blue cheese. Cover and refrigerate at least 4 hours, stirring once or twice. At serving time, toss lightly and spoon into lettuce-lined bowl. Top with avocado slices. Makes 12 servings.

Marinate *Broccoli Vinaigrette* in a large bowl or an oblong baking dish. Then, after draining, top the salad with diced hard-cooked eggs.

Mediterranean Potato Salad

Double the recipe to make 20 servings —

    4 cups cubed, cooked potatoes
    1 16-ounce can whole green beans,
        drained
    1 6-ounce can artichoke hearts,
        drained and halved
    1 small red onion, sliced and
        separated into rings
      Dressing
      Leaf lettuce
    1 cup cherry tomatoes
    ¼ cup pitted ripe olives
    3 hard-cooked eggs, peeled and
        quartered
    1 green pepper, sliced in thin rings
    1 2-ounce can rolled anchovies,
        drained
    ¼ cup snipped parsley

Combine first 5 ingredients. Cover; chill several hours or overnight, stirring occasionally. Drain dressing from vegetables and reserve. Spoon drained vegetables into lettuce-lined bowl. Arrange tomatoes, olives, eggs, pepper, and anchovies atop. Sprinkle with parsley. Pass reserved dressing. Serves 10.

Dressing: Blend together 1⅓ cups salad oil; ⅓ cup tarragon vinegar; 2 tablespoons lemon juice; 1 clove garlic, minced; 2 teaspoons dry mustard; 2 teaspoons salt; ½ teaspoon sugar; and dash pepper.

Broccoli Vinaigrette

Cut the recipe in half to make 6 servings —

    4 10-ounce packages frozen broccoli
        spears
    1 cup salad oil
    ⅓ cup vinegar
    ⅓ cup lemon juice
    1 tablespoon sugar
    1½ teaspoons salt
    1½ teaspoons paprika
    1½ teaspoons dry mustard
    ½ teaspoon dried oregano, crushed
      Dash cayenne
    ⅔ cup finely chopped dill pickle
    ⅔ cup minced green pepper
    ⅓ cup snipped parsley
    1 2¼-ounce jar capers, drained
        (¼ cup)
    4 hard-cooked eggs, diced

Cook frozen broccoli spears according to package directions; drain. In screw-top jar combine salad oil, vinegar, lemon juice, sugar, salt, paprika, dry mustard, crushed oregano, cayenne, finely chopped dill pickle, minced green pepper, snipped parsley, and drained capers. Cover and shake vigorously to blend. Pour dressing over broccoli spears; chill overnight. Drain off liquid. Arrange on serving plate. Top with diced eggs. Garnish with sawtooth-cut hard-cooked eggs filled with sieved egg yolks, if desired. Makes 12 servings.

Blue Cheese-Sauced Corn

A quick, tasty vegetable dish —

    3 10-ounce packages frozen whole
        kernel corn
    1 8-ounce carton blue cheese dip
    ¼ cup milk
    2 teaspoons instant minced onion

Cook corn according to package directions. Meanwhile, in saucepan combine blue cheese dip, milk, and instant minced onion. Heat and stir over low heat just till warm. Pour over hot drained corn, stirring gently to coat. Season to taste. Serves 10 to 12.

Easy Cheese-Mushroom Sauce

Serve over your favorite cooked vegetable —

¼ cup finely chopped onion
3 tablespoons finely chopped green
   pepper
2 tablespoons butter or margarine
1 10½-ounce can condensed cream of
   mushroom soup
1 11-ounce can condensed Cheddar
   cheese soup
¼ cup milk
1 teaspoon dry mustard

In saucepan cook onion and green pepper in butter or margarine till tender but not brown. Stir in soups, milk, and dry mustard. Heat through. Serve over hot, drained vegetables. Makes about 2¾ cups sauce.

Cheesy Potato Bake

Cut the recipe in half to make 8 servings —

16 medium potatoes, peeled and
   thinly sliced (16 cups)
⅔ cup chopped onion
3 10½-ounce cans condensed cream of
   mushroom soup
8 ounces sharp process American
   cheese, shredded (2 cups)
1½ cups milk
½ teaspoon salt
⅛ teaspoon pepper
2 cups soft bread crumbs
4 ounces sharp process American
   cheese, shredded (1 cup)
2 tablespoons butter or margarine,
   melted

Spread *4 cups* of the potatoes in bottom of *each* of two greased 2½-quart casseroles. Combine onion, soup, 8 ounces cheese, milk, salt, and pepper. Pour one-fourth of the soup mixture over potatoes in *each* casserole. Repeat layers. Cover; bake at 350° for 1 hour. Combine bread crumbs, 4 ounces cheese, and melted butter or margarine. Uncover casseroles; sprinkle with bread crumb mixture. Bake 45 minutes longer. Makes 16 servings.

Baked Bean Quintet

6 slices bacon
1 cup chopped onion
1 clove garlic, minced
1 16-ounce can kidney beans, drained
1 16-ounce can green lima beans,
   drained
1 16-ounce can butter beans, drained
1 15-ounce can garbanzo beans,
   drained
1 14-ounce jar or 16-ounce can baked
   beans in molasses sauce
¾ cup catsup
¼ cup brown sugar
½ teaspoon dry mustard
¼ teaspoon pepper

Cook bacon in skillet till crisp; remove and crumble. Cook onion and garlic in bacon drippings till tender but not brown. Combine with beans, catsup, brown sugar, dry mustard, pepper, and crumbled bacon in 3-quart casserole. Bake, covered, at 375° till heated through, about 1 to 1¼ hours. Makes 14 servings.

Savory Vegetable Trio

3 cups sliced yellow summer squash
   (about ¾ pound)
1 9-ounce package frozen cut green
   beans
½ cup water
½ cup chopped onion
¼ cup snipped parsley
1½ teaspoons salt
¼ teaspoon dried thyme, crushed
¼ teaspoon ground sage
⅛ teaspoon pepper
• • •
2 large tomatoes, peeled and cut
   in wedges
2 tablespoons butter or margarine

In large saucepan combine squash, beans, water, onion, parsley, salt, thyme, sage, and pepper. Bring to boiling. Cover; reduce heat and simmer till vegetables are tender, about 10 minutes. Drain thoroughly. Add tomatoes and butter or margarine; cover and heat through. Makes 10 to 12 servings.

Cheesecake Bread Ring

  1 package hot roll mix
  ¼ cup sugar
  1 egg
  ½ cup dairy sour cream
  6 tablespoons butter, melted
    Cream Cheese Filling

Soften yeast from roll mix in ¼ cup warm water. Combine roll mix and sugar. Stir in the yeast, egg, sour cream, and butter; mix well. Place dough in greased bowl, turning once to grease surface. Cover; chill 2 to 3 hours. Turn out onto lightly floured surface. Roll dough to an 18-inch circle. Gently fit into 6½-cup ring mold, allowing dough to cover center and some to hang over edges.

Pour Cream Cheese Filling into mold. Bring dough from sides over top of filling; seal to center of mold. Cut an "X" in dough covering center hole; fold the four triangles back over top of ring, sealing to outer edges. Let rise till almost double, 1 to 1½ hours. Bake at 350° till wooden pick inserted into filling comes out clean, 35 to 40 minutes. Cool in pan 10 minutes; turn out on rack. Sprinkle lightly with confectioners' sugar, if desired. Makes 10 to 12 servings.

Cream Cheese Filling: Beat one 8-ounce package cream cheese, softened; ½ cup sugar; and 1 teaspoon vanilla till smooth. Add 2 eggs, one at a time, beating well after each.

Mustard-Sesame Slices

  ½ cup butter or margarine, softened
  ¼ cup snipped parsley
  2 tablespoons chopped green onion
  2 tablespoons prepared mustard
  1 tablespoon sesame seed, toasted
  1 teaspoon lemon juice
  1 loaf French bread

Blend butter, parsley, onion, mustard, sesame seed, and lemon juice. Slice bread; spread both sides of slices with butter mixture. Arrange on baking sheet and toast at 350° for 20 minutes, *or* reassemble buttered slices into loaf, wrap loosely in foil, and heat at 375° for 10 to 15 minutes.

Brioche

Soften 1 package active dry yeast in ¼ cup warm water. Scald ½ cup milk; cool to lukewarm. Thoroughly cream ½ cup butter or margarine, ⅓ cup sugar, and ½ teaspoon salt. Add lukewarm milk. Add 1 cup sifted all-purpose flour to creamed mixture. Add softened yeast, 3 beaten eggs, and 1 beaten egg yolk; beat well. Add 2¼ cups sifted all-purpose flour; beat 5 to 8 minutes longer. Cover; let rise till double, about 2 hours. Stir down; beat well. Cover; refrigerate overnight.

Stir down; turn out on lightly floured surface. Divide dough in fourths. Set aside ¼ of dough. Halve remaining 3 pieces; form each half into 4 balls (24 in all). Place balls in greased muffin pans. Cut reserved dough into 4 wedges; divide and shape each into 6 small balls (24 in all). Make indentation in top of dough in muffin pans; brush with water. Press small ball into each indentation. Cover; let rise till double, about 1 hour. Combine 1 slightly beaten egg white and 1 tablespoon sugar; brush tops. Bake at 375° for 15 minutes. Serve warm. Makes 24 buns.

Manna Bread

In mixer bowl combine 2 packages active dry yeast, 1¾ cups sifted all-purpose flour, and ¼ cup dry onion soup mix. Cook 8 slices bacon till crisp; drain, reserving 2 tablespoons drippings. Crumble bacon; set aside. Heat together one 12-ounce can beer, ¼ cup milk, 1 tablespoon sugar, and reserved drippings just till warm (mixture will appear curdled). Add to dry ingredients. Beat at low speed of electric mixer for ½ minute. Beat 3 minutes at high speed of electric mixer.

Stir in crumbled bacon and 2 to 2¼ cups sifted all-purpose flour to make moderately stiff dough. Knead till smooth and elastic. Place in greased bowl, turning once to grease surface. Cover; let rise till almost double, 40 to 45 minutes. Punch down. Shape into 16 rolls. Place in two 9x1½-inch round baking pans. Brush with melted butter; sprinkle with yellow cornmeal. Cover lightly; let rise till almost double, about 25 minutes. Bake at 375° for 20 minutes. Makes 16 rolls.

Cream-of-Potato Soup Bread

In mixer bowl combine 2 packages active dry yeast and 2½ cups sifted all-purpose flour. Heat 1½ cups milk, 2 tablespoons *each* butter and sugar, and 2 teaspoons salt till warm; add to dry ingredients. Add one 10½-ounce can condensed cream of potato soup. Beat at low speed of electric mixer for ½ minute, scraping sides. Beat 3 minutes at high speed. By hand, stir in 3 to 3½ cups sifted all-purpose flour to make moderately stiff dough.

Turn out onto lightly floured surface. Knead till smooth, 5 to 8 minutes. Place in greased bowl, turning once. Cover; let rise till double. Punch down. Cover; let rest 10 minutes. Divide in half; shape into two loaves. Place in two greased 8½x4½x2½-inch loaf dishes. Let rise till double. Bake at 400° till done, 25 to 30 minutes. Makes 2 loaves.

Raisin-Nut Bread

1 cup raisins
1 beaten egg
¾ cup sugar
½ teaspoon vanilla
1½ cups sifted all-purpose flour
1 teaspoon baking powder
¼ teaspoon baking soda
½ cup chopped walnuts

In saucepan combine raisins and 1 cup water; bring to boil. Cool to room temperature. Mix egg, sugar, and vanilla; stir in raisin mixture. Sift together flour, baking powder, baking soda, and ¼ teaspoon salt. Add to egg-raisin mixture, beating well. Stir in nuts. Pour into 2 greased and floured 16-ounce fruit or vegetable cans. Bake at 350° till done, 50 to 60 minutes. Makes 2 loaves.

Homemade bread is always a big hit with guests, especially when it is as tasty as this beer- and bacon-flavored *Manna Bread*. For extra deliciousness serve it warm.

Give the top of *Chocolate Éclair Cake* a pretty weblike look by drawing a knife through the soft icing at regular intervals.

Sauerkraut Surprise Cake

½ cup butter or margarine
1½ cups sugar
3 eggs
1 teaspoon vanilla
2 cups sifted all-purpose flour
½ cup cocoa powder
1 teaspoon baking powder
1 teaspoon baking soda
1 8-ounce can sauerkraut, drained
Choco Frosting

Cream butter and sugar till light. Beat in eggs, one at a time; add vanilla. Sift next 4 ingredients and ¼ teaspoon salt; add to creamed mixture alternately with 1 cup water, beating after each addition. Rinse and finely snip kraut; stir into cocoa mixture. Turn into greased and floured 13x9x2-inch baking pan. Bake at 350° for 35 to 40 minutes. Cool. Frost with Choco Frosting. Serves 12 to 16.

Choco Frosting: Melt one 6-ounce package semisweet chocolate pieces and ¼ cup butter over low heat. Remove from heat; blend in ½ cup dairy sour cream, 1 teaspoon vanilla, and ¼ teaspoon salt. Gradually add sifted confectioners' sugar (2½ to 2¾ cups) to make of spreading consistency; beat well.

Chocolate Éclair Cake

4 1-ounce squares unsweetened
   chocolate, melted
½ cup boiling water
1¾ cups sugar
2¼ cups sifted cake flour
3 teaspoons baking powder
½ cup salad oil
7 egg yolks
¾ cup cold water
1 teaspoon vanilla
7 egg whites
½ teaspoon cream of tartar
   Custard Filling
   Chocolate Icing
   Confectioners' Sugar Icing

Combine chocolate, boiling water, and ¼ *cup* sugar; cool. Sift together flour, remaining sugar, baking powder, and 1 teaspoon salt into bowl. Make well in center of dry ingredients. Add, in order, next 4 ingredients. Beat smooth. Stir in chocolate mixture. In large mixer bowl combine egg whites and cream of tartar; beat till very stiff peaks form. Pour chocolate mixture in thin stream over entire surface of whites; fold in gently. Bake in ungreased 10-inch tube pan at 325° for 65 minutes. Invert pan to cool; remove from pan.

Prepare Custard Filling. Using wooden picks for guides, split cake into 3 layers. Fill between layers with Custard Filling. Frost with Chocolate Icing. Immediately pipe Confectioners' Sugar Icing around top; draw knife through icing at regular intervals to give web effect. Chill. Serves 12 to 16.

· *Custard Filling:* In saucepan combine ¼ cup sugar and ¼ cup cornstarch. Stir in 3 cups milk; stir in 2 beaten eggs. Cook and stir till thickened and bubbly; add 2 teaspoons vanilla. Cover surface with waxed paper; cool.

Chocolate Icing: In saucepan melt together one 4-ounce package sweet cooking chocolate and 3 tablespoons butter over low heat. Remove from heat; stir in 1½ cups sifted confectioners' sugar and enough hot water (3 to 4 tablespoons) to make of pouring consistency.

Confectioners' Sugar Icing: Add enough light cream to 1 cup sifted confectioners' sugar to make of spreading consistency. Add dash salt and ½ teaspoon vanilla.

Tantalize guests with *Chocolate Éclair Cake.* To assemble this rich dessert, cut the chiffon cake into thirds and spread the custard filling between the layers. Then, add the icing.

Orange Rum-Yum Cake

2 17-ounce packages pound cake mix
2 tablespoons shredded orange peel
2 teaspoons shredded lemon peel
1 cup sugar
1 cup orange juice
3 tablespoons lemon juice
2 tablespoons rum

Prepare cake mixes together according to package directions, adding orange peel and lemon peel. Turn into greased and lightly floured 10-inch fluted tube pan. Bake at 350° till done, about 1 to 1¼ hours. Cool in pan 10 minutes. Remove from pan to cooling rack; cool 20 minutes more. Place on serving plate. Using long-tined fork or skewer, punch holes in top of cake at 1-inch intervals. Combine remaining ingredients; bring to boiling. Spoon syrup *very slowly* over cake, allowing cake to absorb sauce; continue till all the syrup is used. Chill. Makes 12 to 16 servings.

Jamocha Mousse

Cut the recipe in half to make 8 servings —

2 6-ounce packages semisweet chocolate pieces
8 egg yolks
⅓ cup rum
1 tablespoon instant coffee powder
8 egg whites
Dash salt
1 cup sugar
Frozen whipped dessert topping, thawed

Reserve a few chocolate pieces for garnish. In heavy saucepan melt remaining chocolate pieces over *very low heat.* Add egg yolks, one at a time, beating after each addition. Remove from heat. Blend in rum and coffee powder. Beat egg whites and salt till frothy; gradually add sugar, beating to stiff peaks. Stir a small amount of beaten egg whites into chocolate mixture; fold into remaining egg whites. Spoon into 16 sherbets or dessert dishes; chill. Garnish with whipped topping and reserved chocolate pieces. Serves 16.

Fresh Fruit Bars

1 roll refrigerated sugar cookie dough
1 8-ounce package cream cheese, softened
⅓ cup sugar
½ teaspoon vanilla
• • •
2 cups sliced peaches
2 cups raspberries
¼ cup apricot preserves *or* orange marmalade
1 tablespoon water

Cut refrigerated sugar cookie dough into ⅛-inch thick slices. Arrange cookie dough in bottom of ungreased 15½x10½x1-inch baking pan *or* 14-inch pizza pan, overlapping edges of dough slightly. Press to even dough. Bake at 375° for 12 minutes; cool.

In mixer bowl combine cream cheese, sugar, and vanilla; beat till smooth. Spread on cooled cookie crust; arrange peaches and raspberries on top. Combine preserves or marmalade and water; spoon over fruits. Chill. Cut into 3x2-inch bars or diamonds. Makes 25 bars.

Homemade Raspberry Ice Cream

1 3-ounce package raspberry-flavored gelatin
½ cup boiling water
1 10-ounce package frozen raspberries, thawed and sieved
• • •
2 eggs
1 cup whipping cream
1 3¾- or 3⅝-ounce package *instant* vanilla pudding mix
⅔ cup sugar
2 teaspoons vanilla
1 quart milk

In mixing bowl dissolve raspberry-flavored gelatin in boiling water; stir in sieved raspberries. Beat eggs; add whipping cream, dry pudding mix, sugar, and vanilla. Stir into raspberry mixture. Pour into 1-gallon ice cream freezer container; add milk and stir till blended. Freeze according to freezer manufacturer's directions. Makes 2 quarts.

Sundae Special

Double the recipe for larger groups —

1 12-ounce package semisweet
    chocolate pieces (2 cups)
1 cup miniature marshmallows
¼ cup light corn syrup
    • • •
1 7-ounce bottle lemon-lime carbonated
    beverage (about 1 cup)
1 teaspoon vanilla
    Vanilla or peppermint ice cream

In heavy saucepan combine semisweet chocolate pieces, miniature marshmallows, and light corn syrup. Cook and stir till chocolate and marshmallows are melted. Remove from heat; gradually stir in lemon-lime carbonated beverage. Add vanilla. Serve over vanilla or peppermint ice cream. Makes 2⅓ cups sauce.

Fluffy Pineapple Dessert

A light, yet rich dessert —

3 cups fine vanilla wafer crumbs
½ cup butter or margarine, melted
    • • •
1¼ cups sugar
3 envelopes unflavored gelatin
    Dash salt
1½ cups pineapple juice
1 20½-ounce can crushed pineapple
2 slightly beaten egg whites
1½ cups whipping cream
¾ cup chopped pecans

Mix together vanilla wafer crumbs and melted butter. Press firmly into bottom of 13½x8¾x 1¾-inch baking dish. Chill till set. In saucepan combine sugar, gelatin, and salt. Add pineapple juice; cook and stir till boiling. Remove from heat; stir in undrained crushed pineapple. Cool to room temperature; stir in egg whites. Chill till mixture is partially set. Beat at high speed of electric mixer till light and fluffy, 6 to 8 minutes. Whip cream. Fold whipped cream and chopped nuts into gelatin mixture; spoon over vanilla wafer crust. Chill till firm. Makes 14 to 16 servings.

Ice Cream Sundae Mold

¼ cup flaked coconut, toasted
1½ teaspoons brandy flavoring
1 quart vanilla ice cream, softened
1 quart coffee ice cream, softened
¼ cup slivered almonds, toasted
1 6-ounce package semisweet
    chocolate pieces
⅔ cup light corn syrup
1 6-ounce can evaporated milk

Stir coconut and brandy flavoring into vanilla ice cream; turn into 6½-cup mold and freeze till firm. Stir together coffee ice cream and almonds; spoon into mold atop vanilla layer. Freeze firm, about 5 hours.

Meanwhile, to prepare sauce, combine chocolate pieces and syrup in saucepan. Cook and stir over low heat till chocolate melts. Cool. Gradually stir in evaporated milk.

Unmold firm ice cream mixture onto serving plate. Drizzle with sauce; sprinkle with additional almonds, if desired. Pass remaining sauce. Makes 10 to 12 servings.

Lemon-Sour Cream Tarts

3 sticks piecrust mix
2 cups canned lemon pie filling
1 cup dairy sour cream
1 10-ounce package frozen raspberries,
    thawed
2 tablespoons sugar
1 tablespoon cornstarch

Prepare piecrust mix according to directions. Roll *half* the dough ⅛ inch thick; cut in five 5-inch circles. Fit into tart pans. Repeat with remaining half of dough. Trim ½ inch beyond edge; turn under and flute. Prick bottom and sides well with fork. Bake at 450° for 10 to 12 minutes. Cool.

Stir together pie filling and sour cream; chill. Drain raspberries, reserving ⅔ cup syrup. Mix sugar and cornstarch in small saucepan; gradually stir in reserved syrup. Cook and stir till thickened and bubbly; chill. Fill tart shells with lemon mixture; top with a few berries. Spoon about 1 tablespoon glaze over each. Makes 10 tarts.

MENUS

```
MAKE-AHEAD BRUNCH (16)

Chilled Fruit Cup
Cheesy Egg-Bacon Bake
Orange-Chocolate Rolls    Butter
Coffee    Milk
```

Entertain the easy way with a brunch that stresses advance preparation. Set the table and prepare the food a day ahead. Then, all you need to do the morning of the brunch is warm the casserole and rolls and make the coffee.

Cheesy Egg-Bacon Bake

¼ cup finely chopped onion
½ cup butter or margarine
½ cup all-purpose flour
4 cups milk
6 ounces process Swiss cheese, shredded (1½ cups)
1 cup diced Canadian bacon
⅓ cup chopped canned pimiento
16 hard-cooked eggs, quartered
1½ cups soft bread crumbs
3 tablespoons butter, melted
Toast points

Advance preparation: In saucepan cook onion in ½ cup butter till tender. Blend in flour, ½ teaspoon salt, and ⅛ teaspoon pepper. Add milk; cook and stir till bubbly. Add cheese, bacon, and pimiento; stir till cheese melts. Place *half* the eggs in bottom of 3-quart casserole. Spoon *half* the sauce over. Repeat layers. Cover; chill up to 24 hours. Toss crumbs with melted butter; wrap and chill.

Before serving: Bake casserole at 375° for 45 minutes. Sprinkle with crumbs. Bake about 15 minutes more. Serve over toast. Serves 16.

Orange-Chocolate Rolls

1 package active dry yeast
3½ cups sifted all-purpose flour
1¼ cups milk
¼ cup granulated sugar
¼ cup shortening
1 teaspoon salt
1 egg
½ cup granulated sugar
¼ cup butter or margarine, melted
1 tablespoon grated orange peel
½ cup semisweet chocolate pieces
• • •
2 cups sifted confectioners' sugar
Orange juice
1 teaspoon vanilla

Advance preparation: In mixer bowl combine yeast and 2¼ *cups* of the flour. Heat milk, ¼ cup granulated sugar, shortening, and salt till warm, stirring occasionally to melt shortening. Add to dry ingredients in mixer bowl; add egg. Beat at low speed of electric mixer for ½ minute, scraping sides of bowl. Beat 3 minutes at high speed. Stir in enough of the remaining flour to make soft dough. Place in greased bowl, turning once. Cover; let rise till double, 1½ to 2 hours.

Turn dough out on lightly floured surface; divide in half. Roll *each half* to 16x8-inch rectangle. Combine ½ cup granulated sugar, melted butter, and orange peel; spread *half* the sugar mixture over each rectangle. Top each with *half* of the chocolate pieces. Roll up jelly-roll fashion. Seal edge; cut each roll into 16 slices. Place slices, cut side down, in two greased 9x9x2-inch baking pans. Cover; let rise till double, about 30 to 40 minutes. Bake at 375° for 20 to 25 minutes. Cool on rack. Wrap in foil; freeze.

Before serving: Thaw frozen rolls. Heat in foil wrap at 375° for 15 minutes. Meanwhile, combine confectioners' sugar with enough orange juice to make of spreading consistency (about 2 tablespoons). Stir in vanilla. Drizzle over warm rolls. Makes 32 rolls.

Prevent last-minute work by making *Orange-Chocolate Rolls* in advance and freezing them.   At serving time, simply reheat the rolls and drizzle with orange-flavored icing.

```
┌─────────────────────────┐
│   LADIES' LUNCHEON (12) │
│                         │
│  Crab-Sauced Cheese Pie │
│  Buttered Asparagus for 12 │
│  Spicy Peaches   Relishes │
│  Cranberry Ambrosia     │
│     Coffee    Tea       │
└─────────────────────────┘
```

Don't save your good china and linens just for nighttime entertaining. Bring them out for this noon luncheon, one that features a rich cheese pie served with a creamy crab sauce. In fact, go all out. Pay close attention to the placement of china, silverware, glassware, and napkins, and accent the table setting with a dainty bouquet of flowers. This combination of pretty table setting and delicious food is sure to impress your luncheon guests.

Buttered Asparagus for 12

Cook four 10-ounce packages frozen asparagus spears in boiling, salted water according to package directions. Avoid overcooking the asparagus so that it remains a bright green color. Melt ¼ cup butter. Drain asparagus and drizzle with melted butter. Serves 12.

Spicy Peaches

     2 29-ounce cans peach halves
     ½ cup sugar
     ⅓ cup vinegar
     6 inches stick cinnamon
     ½ teaspoon whole cloves

Drain peaches reserving 1½ cups syrup. In large saucepan combine reserved syrup, sugar, vinegar, cinnamon, and cloves; heat, stirring constantly, till sugar dissolves and mixture boils. Simmer, uncovered, for 5 minutes. Add peach halves; simmer 15 minutes, turning peach halves occasionally. Chill at least overnight. Makes 12 servings.

Crab-Sauced Cheese Pie

Deliciously rich—

     2¼ cups sifted all-purpose flour
     3 tablespoons milk
     ⅔ cup salad oil
     8 slightly beaten egg yolks
     2 cups light cream
     1 cup milk
     ¼ teaspoon ground nutmeg
     8 egg whites
     12 ounces natural Swiss cheese,
        shredded (3 cups)
        Crab Sauce
        Paprika

Sift together flour and 1 teaspoon salt. Combine milk and oil; stir into dry ingredients till just mixed. Pat into the bottom and 1 inch up the sides of a 13½x8¾x1¾-inch baking dish. Bake at 450° till lightly browned, about 10 minutes; remove from oven. Reduce oven temperature to 350°. Combine egg yolks, light cream, milk, 1 teaspoon salt, and nutmeg. Beat egg whites till stiff peaks form; fold into yolks. Fold in cheese. Pour into crust. Bake at 350° till knife inserted just off-center comes out clean, 30 to 35 minutes. Let stand 5 minutes before cutting. Serve with Crab Sauce. Sprinkle with paprika. Makes 12 servings.

Crab Sauce: Heat two 7½-ounce cans crab meat, drained, flaked, and cartilage removed, in ¼ cup butter or margarine. Blend in ¼ cup all-purpose flour and ½ teaspoon salt. Add 2 cups light cream; cook and stir till mixture is thickened and bubbly.

Cranberry Ambrosia

     6 large oranges, peeled and sliced
     4 large fully ripe bananas, sliced
     1 16-ounce can jellied cranberry
        sauce, chilled and cubed
     ¾ cup flaked coconut
     2 cups catawba grape juice

Halve orange slices. Carefully toss together oranges, bananas, and cranberry cubes. Sprinkle flaked coconut over top. Pour catawba juice over all. Makes 12 servings.

Baked Bananas

Peel 14 firm ripe bananas; dip in ¼ cup lemon juice. Brush bananas with ¼ cup butter or margarine, melted. Sprinkle with salt. Wrap each banana in foil; bake at 325° till fork will pierce banana easily, about 25 minutes. To serve, fold foil back; sprinkle with paprika and garnish with parsley sprigs. Makes 14 servings.

Fresh Coconut Cake

> 1 fresh coconut
> ⅔ cup shortening
> ½ teaspoon grated lime peel
> 1½ cups sugar
> 3 eggs
> 2¼ cups sifted all-purpose flour
> 2½ teaspoons baking powder
> 2 tablespoons lime juice
> Fluffy Frosting

Pierce coconut eyes; drain, reserving liquid. Crack shell by tapping with hammer; remove shell. Peel off brown covering. Coarsely chop ¾ cup of the coconut meat. Measure reserved liquid; add water to make ¾ cup liquid. Heat liquid. Place chopped coconut meat and hot liquid in blender container. Cover and blend till almost smooth. Set aside.

Mix shortening and lime peel. Gradually add sugar; cream till fluffy. Add eggs, one at a time, beating well after each. Sift together flour, baking powder, and ½ teaspoon salt. Add to creamed mixture alternately with lime juice and coconut mixture; beat well after each addition. Turn into 2 greased and lightly floured 9x1½-inch round pans. Bake at 375° for 25 to 30 minutes. Cool 10 minutes; remove from pans. Cool. Frost with Fluffy Frosting. Garnish with shredded fresh coconut, if desired. Makes 14 servings.

Fluffy Frosting: Combine 1 cup sugar, ¼ cup water, ¼ teaspoon cream of tartar, and dash salt in saucepan. Bring to boiling, stirring till sugar dissolves. Very slowly add sugar syrup to 2 unbeaten egg whites in mixer bowl, beating constantly with electric mixer till stiff peaks form, about 7 minutes. Beat in 1 tablespoon lime juice and 1 teaspoon vanilla. Spread at once on the cooled cake.

POLYNESIAN DINNER (14)

Teriyaki Roast Beef
Green Beans
Baked Bananas
Tropical Fruit Assortment
Fresh Coconut Cake
Pineapple Juice   Tea

Bring the charm of the tropical islands to your home by having a Polynesian-style dinner. In addition to the delicious food, create a Polynesian mood for this party. Start by covering a low table (preferably outdoors) with broad green leaves. Then, add some bright-colored hibiscus or orchids and a few fresh pineapples. And be sure to wear a gaily printed outfit. Round out the mood with hula music in the background.

Teriyaki Roast Beef

> 1 cup soy sauce
> ½ cup salad oil
> ¼ cup molasses
> 1 tablespoon ground ginger
> 1 tablespoon dry mustard
> 8 cloves garlic, minced
> 1 6- to 7-pound boneless beef rib
>   roast

To make the marinade, mix soy, salad oil, molasses, ground ginger, dry mustard, and garlic. Add meat to marinade, turning to coat. Refrigerate overnight, spooning marinade over occasionally. Drain, reserving marinade. Place meat on rack in shallow roasting pan. Insert meat thermometer. Basting several times with marinade, roast meat at 325° till thermometer registers 140° for rare, 160° for medium, or 170° for well-done. Allow about 3 hours for rare, about 4 hours for medium, and about 4¾ hours for well-done. Remove roast from oven; cover with foil and let set 15 minutes before carving. Makes 14 servings.

HOLIDAY DINNER (12)

Elegant Stuffed Turkey*
Apricot-Sauced Sweets   Deluxe Peas
Twinberry Salad
Butterhorns*   Butter
Pumpkin Cheesecake*
or
Frozen Pumpkin Squares*
Coffee   Milk

Holidays customarily mean getting together with family or friends for a feast. When it's your turn to host the celebration, serve a menu that offers traditional foods in some not-so-traditional ways. For example, the turkey is stuffed with an oyster-rice stuffing, and the pumpkin can be served as either a frozen dessert or as a baked pumpkin cheesecake. You'll have fun discovering the new flavors.

Deluxe Peas

3 10-ounce packages frozen peas
1 cup chopped onion
¼ cup butter or margarine
1 6-ounce can sliced mushrooms, drained
¼ cup chopped canned pimiento
1 tablespoon sugar
1 teaspoon salt

Cook peas according to package directions; drain. Cook onion in butter till tender but not brown. Add peas, mushrooms, and pimiento. Stir in sugar, salt, and ⅛ teaspoon pepper. Cover and heat through. Makes 12 servings.

Hearty fare

← Accompany the *Elegant Stuffed Turkey* with *Apricot-Sauced Sweets, Deluxe Peas, Twinberry Salad,* and homemade *Butterhorns.*

Apricot-Sauced Sweets

Next time, serve these with ham —

1 cup snipped dried apricots
¾ cup orange juice
½ cup water
3 tablespoons brown sugar
2 tablespoons honey
2 tablespoons butter or margarine
2½ pounds sweet potatoes, cooked, peeled, and cut crosswise in thick pieces
½ cup walnut halves

In saucepan combine apricots, orange juice, water, brown sugar, and honey. Bring to boiling; cover and simmer till apricots are tender, about 20 to 25 minutes. Remove from heat and stir in butter. Arrange sweet potatoes in 12-inch skillet; sprinkle with walnuts. Pour apricot sauce over. Cover and simmer till potatoes are heated through and glazed, about 15 minutes. Baste frequently. Serves 12.

Twinberry Salad

Apple and celery add a crunchy texture —

3 3-ounce packages strawberry-flavored gelatin
3 cups boiling water
2 16-ounce cans whole cranberry sauce
3 tablespoons lemon juice
2 cups chopped unpeeled apple
1 cup chopped celery
½ cup whipping cream
½ cup mayonnaise or salad dressing
Lettuce

Dissolve gelatin in boiling water. Stir in whole cranberry sauce and lemon juice; chill till partially set. Fold in apple and celery. Turn into 13½x8¾x1¾-inch dish; chill till firm. Whip cream; fold in mayonnaise. Cut salad into squares and serve on lettuce-lined plates. Top with a dollop of the whipped cream-mayonnaise dressing. Makes 12 servings.

Recipes on next page.

Elegant Stuffed Turkey

    2 slightly beaten eggs
    1 10¼-ounce can condensed oyster stew
    1 6-ounce package long grain and
        wild rice mix
    1 7-ounce package herb-seasoned
        stuffing cubes
            • • •
    1 14-pound ready-to-cook turkey

Combine eggs, stew, and ⅓ cup water. Cook rice mix following package directions; cool. Add rice and stuffing cubes to stew; toss. Stuff bird; truss. Place bird, breast up, in roasting pan. Cover with "tent" of foil. Roast at 325° till meat thermometer registers 185°, about 5 to 5½ hours. Serves 12.

Butterhorns

    1 package active dry yeast
    4½ to 4¾ cups sifted all-purpose flour
    1 cup milk
    ½ cup sugar
    ½ cup shortening
    3 beaten eggs
      Melted butter or margarine

In large mixer bowl combine yeast and *2¾ cups* of the sifted flour. Heat milk, sugar, shortening, and 2 teaspoons salt just till warm, stirring occasionally. Add to dry ingredients in mixer bowl; add eggs. Beat at low speed with electric mixer for ½ minute, scraping sides of bowl constantly. Beat 3 minutes at high speed. By hand, stir in enough of the remaining flour to make soft dough. Turn out onto lightly floured surface; knead till smooth and elastic, 5 to 8 minutes.

Place dough in greased bowl, turning once. Cover; let rise till double, 2½ hours. Turn onto lightly floured surface. Divide dough into thirds; roll each third to 12-inch circle.

Brush circles with melted butter. Cut each circle into 12 pie-shaped wedges. Beginning at wide end of wedge, roll toward point. Arrange rolls, point down, on greased baking sheets; brush with melted butter. Cover and let rise till double, about 1 hour. Bake at 400° for 10 to 12 minutes. Makes 36.

Pumpkin Cheesecake

      Zwieback Crust
    2 8-ounce packages cream cheese,
        softened
    1 cup light cream
    1 cup canned pumpkin
    ¾ cup sugar
    4 egg yolks
    3 tablespoons all-purpose flour
    1 teaspoon vanilla
    1 teaspoon ground cinnamon
    ½ teaspoon ground ginger
    ½ teaspoon ground nutmeg
    4 stiffly beaten egg whites
    1 cup dairy sour cream
    2 tablespoons sugar
    ½ teaspoon vanilla

Zwieback Crust: Combine 1½ cups zwieback crumbs, 3 tablespoons sugar, and 3 tablespoons butter or margarine, melted. Press into bottom and 2 inches up sides of 9-inch springform pan. Bake at 325° for 5 minutes.

For filling combine cream cheese, next 9 ingredients, and ¼ teaspoon salt in large mixer bowl. Beat till smooth. Fold in egg whites. Turn into prepared Zwieback Crust. Bake at 325° for 1 hour. Combine remaining ingredients; spread over cheesecake. Bake 5 minutes more. Chill thoroughly. Serves 12.

Frozen Pumpkin Squares

    1 16-ounce can pumpkin (2 cups)
    1 cup sugar
    1 teaspoon ground ginger
    1 teaspoon ground cinnamon
    ½ teaspoon ground nutmeg
    1 cup chopped pecans, toasted
    ½ gallon vanilla ice cream, softened
   36 gingersnaps

Combine first 5 ingredients and 1 teaspoon salt; add pecans. In chilled bowl fold pumpkin mixture into ice cream. Line bottom of 13x9x2-inch pan with *half* the gingersnaps; top with *half* the pumpkin mixture. Repeat layers. Freeze till firm, about 5 hours. Cut in squares; garnish with whipped cream and pecan halves, if desired. Makes 12 servings.

```
┌─────────────────────────────┐
│      BUFFET DINNER (12)      │
│                             │
│   Rib Roast with Onion Butter │
│        Curried Rice         │
│    Buttered Broccoli Spears │
│ Fruit Salad Plate   Orange Dressing │
│      Vegetable Relishes     │
│        Rolls    Butter      │
│      Mocha Cream Puffs      │
│        Coffee    Tea        │
└─────────────────────────────┘
```

Ever thought of making the salad do double duty as a centerpiece? Try it when you serve this buffet. Choose a pretty plate or shallow bowl and a colorful assortment of fruits. Then, arrange the fruits attractively and center the salad on the buffet table as shown on page 46.

Mocha Cream Puffs

½ cup butter or margarine
1 cup boiling water
1 cup sifted all-purpose flour
¼ teaspoon salt
4 eggs
1 17-ounce can chocolate pudding
2 teaspoons instant coffee powder
1 cup whipping cream
   Sifted confectioners' sugar

Melt butter in boiling water. Add flour and salt all at once; stir vigorously. Cook and stir till mixture forms ball that doesn't separate. Remove from heat; cool slightly. Add eggs, one at a time, beating after each till smooth. Drop by heaping tablespoons, 3 inches apart, on greased baking sheet. Bake at 450° for 15 minutes, then at 325° for 25 minutes. Remove from oven; split. Turn oven off; put cream puffs back in to dry, about 20 minutes. Cool thoroughly on rack.

Combine pudding and coffee powder. Whip cream; fold into pudding mixture. Chill. Just before serving, spoon filling into puffs. Dust tops with confectioners' sugar. Makes 12.

Rib Roast with Onion Butter

1 5-pound boneless beef rib roast
   Salt and pepper
¾ cup butter or margarine, softened
¼ cup chopped green onion
1 teaspoon Worcestershire sauce
¼ teaspoon freshly ground pepper

Place meat, fat side up, on rack in shallow roasting pan. Season with salt and pepper. Insert meat thermometer. Roast, uncovered, at 325° till meat thermometer registers 140° for rare, 160° for medium, and 170° for well-done. Allow about 2¾ hours for rare, about 3¼ hours for medium, and about 4 hours for well-done. Meanwhile, blend butter or margarine, green onion, Worcestershire sauce, and pepper. Dab a little butter on each serving of meat. Makes 12 servings.

Curried Rice

½ cup thinly sliced celery
4 teaspoons curry powder
¼ cup butter or margarine
2 cups uncooked long grain rice
4½ cups water
4 beef bouillon cubes, crumbled
1 cup coarsely chopped cashew nuts

In large saucepan cook celery and curry powder in butter or margarine till celery is tender but not brown. Add rice and cook till yellow but not brown. Stir in water, crumbled bouillon cubes, and ½ teaspoon salt. Cover and bring to boiling. Reduce heat and simmer, covered, till rice is tender, 20 to 25 minutes. Just before serving, add cashews and toss lightly to mix. Makes 12 servings.

Orange Dressing

In saucepan combine *half* of a 6-ounce can frozen orange juice concentrate, thawed (⅓ cup); ¼ cup sugar; ¼ cup water; and 2 beaten eggs. Cook and stir over low heat till thickened. Cool. Whip ½ cup whipping cream. Fold whipped cream and ½ cup mayonnaise into cooled mixture. Chill. Makes 2½ cups.

ITALIAN DINNER (14)

Spaghetti and Meatballs
Tossed Zucchini Salad
Jiffy Breadsticks
Easy Zabaglione with Peaches
Chianti   Coffee

Get out the checked tablecloth and napkins and have an Italian-inspired dinner. For the centerpiece, use a multicolored candle in a raffia-covered bottle. Or gather together a handful of long strands of uncooked spaghetti with a bright red ribbon. Lay the bundle in the center of the table and flank both ends of the centerpiece with tall candles.

To simplify serving, dish up the spaghetti in the kitchen. Top each serving with three meatballs, then ladle about ½ cup sauce over meat and cooked pasta. Pass extra Parmesan cheese in a decorative cheese shaker.

Easy Zabaglione with Peaches

    2 3½-ounce packages vanilla whipped
        dessert mix
    2 eggs
    ½ cup sugar
    ½ cup dry sherry
    2 29-ounce cans peach slices, well
        drained

In large mixer bowl thoroughly blend dessert mix and 1 cup cold water. Whip at highest speed of electric mixer for 1 minute. (Mixture will be quite thick and fluffy.) Add 1½ cups cold water. Whip at high speed till mixture thickens, about 4 minutes; set aside. Beat eggs till thick and lemon-colored, 3 to 5 minutes. Gradually add sugar, beating till mixture is very thick. Blend egg mixture and wine into whipped dessert mix. Chill at least 1 hour. Before serving, stir the mixture till smooth. Serve sauce over well-drained peach slices in sherbets. Makes 14 servings.

Tossed Zucchini Salad

    ⅔ cup salad oil
    ⅓ cup vinegar
    1 tablespoon sugar
    ⅛ teaspoon garlic powder
    2 cups thinly sliced zucchini
    ¼ cup sliced green onion
    1 medium head lettuce, torn (5 cups)
    1 head romaine, torn (3 cups)
    3 tomatoes, cut in wedges

In screw-top jar combine first 4 ingredients, ½ teaspoon salt, and dash pepper; shake well. Pour over zucchini and onion. Chill 1 to 2 hours. In large salad bowl toss lettuce and romaine. Drain zucchini; reserve marinade. Add zucchini to greens with tomatoes. Toss with desired amount of marinade. Serves 14.

Jiffy Breadsticks

Using 2 packages refrigerated Parker House rolls (24 rolls), split each roll in half. Shape each piece into a 6-inch pencillike stick. Place on greased baking sheet. Brush with water. Sprinkle with coarse (Kosher) salt. Place large shallow pan on lower oven rack; fill with boiling water. Bake sticks above water at 400° about 18 minutes. Makes 48.

Shape *Jiffy Breadsticks* by rolling the dough into pencillike sticks. Brush dough with water and sprinkle with coarse salt.

Spaghetti and Meatballs

1½ cups chopped onion
3 small cloves garlic, crushed
3 tablespoons salad oil
2 29-ounce cans tomatoes, cut up
1 12-ounce can tomato paste
4 beef bouillon cubes
2 tablespoons sugar
2 teaspoons dried oregano, crushed
1 teaspoon dried basil, crushed
¼ teaspoon pepper
3 bay leaves
2 6-ounce cans sliced mushrooms, drained
1 tablespoon grated Parmesan cheese
    Meatballs
2 pounds spaghetti, cooked and drained

In large Dutch oven cook onion and garlic in oil till tender but not brown. Stir in next 8 ingredients and 3 cups water. Bring to boiling; reduce heat and simmer, uncovered, 2 hours, stirring occasionally. Remove bay leaves. Add mushrooms and cheese. Simmer till of desired consistency, about 30 minutes more. Meanwhile, prepare Meatballs. To serve, place hot meatballs atop hot spaghetti; spoon sauce over. Pass additional Parmesan cheese, if desired. Makes 14 servings.

Meatballs: Combine 3 beaten eggs, ¾ cup milk, 2 cups soft bread crumbs, ½ cup grated Parmesan cheese, and 1 teaspoon salt. Mix in 2 pounds ground beef and 1 pound Italian sausage. Shape into 42 medium-sized meatballs. Place in shallow baking pans. Bake at 375° till done, 30 to 35 minutes. Drain off fat.

Plan a dinner menu with a foreign theme. Prepare crisp *Jiffy Breadsticks* from refrigerated rolls, and pass them with the popular Italian entrée, *Spaghetti and Meatballs.*

```
┌─────────────────────────────────┐
│                                 │
│      MAKE-AHEAD PICNIC (10)      │
│                                 │
│         Sesame Chicken          │
│       Shoestring Potatoes       │
│    Marinated Vegetable Combo    │
│   Spiced Peaches    Apple Rings │
│         Date-Malt Chews         │
│            Iced Tea             │
│                                 │
└─────────────────────────────────┘
```

Combine the beauty of an outdoor setting with good food by entertaining picnic-style. At the picnic site start the fun with an activity, such as swimming or a rousing game of volleyball or badminton, and for the younger set, tag. This is bound to stimulate everybody's appetite. Then, set out the food and call your hungry guests to the table.

Marinated Vegetable Combo

Subtly seasoned with dillweed—

    1 16-ounce can whole kernel corn,
       drained
    1 8-ounce can cut green beans,
       drained
    1 8-ounce can peas, drained
    1 8-ounce can lima beans, drained
    ½ cup finely diced green pepper
    ¼ cup chopped canned pimiento
    ¾ cup vinegar
    ½ cup sugar
    ½ cup salad oil
    1 teaspoon salt
    ½ teaspoon dried dillweed, crushed
    ⅛ teaspoon pepper
      Hard-cooked egg wedges

Advance preparation: Combine corn, green beans, peas, lima beans, green pepper, and pimiento. Blend vinegar, sugar, oil, salt, dillweed, and pepper. Stir together vegetables and dressing. Chill several hours or overnight, stirring occasionally. Drain. Garnish with egg wedges. Makes 10 servings.

Sesame Chicken

Carry the chicken to the picnic in an ice chest or insulated container to keep it well chilled—

    1 cup finely crushed saltine crackers
       (about 27)
    ⅓ cup sesame seed, toasted
    1 teaspoon paprika
    ½ teaspoon salt
           • • •
   20 chicken drumsticks
    ⅓ cup evaporated milk
    ¾ cup butter or margarine, melted

Advance preparation: Combine first 4 ingredients. Dip chicken in milk; roll in crumbs. Pour butter into 13½x8¾x1¾-inch baking dish or a jelly roll pan. Place chicken in pan; turn once. Bake at 375° for 70 minutes. Remove from pan. Cover; chill. Serves 10.

Date-Malt Chews

    6 tablespoons butter or margarine
    ¾ cup brown sugar
    2 eggs
    ½ teaspoon vanilla
    ¾ cup sifted all-purpose flour
    ½ cup chocolate malted milk powder
    ½ teaspoon baking powder
    1 cup snipped dates
    ½ cup chopped walnuts
    ½ cup flaked coconut
      Confectioners' sugar *or* Chocolate
      Malt Frosting

Advance preparation: Melt butter. Remove from heat; blend in brown sugar. Beat in eggs, one at a time; add vanilla. Stir in flour, malted milk powder, and baking powder; mix thoroughly. Fold in dates, nuts, and coconut. Turn into greased and floured 9x9x2-inch baking pan. Bake at 350° for 25 to 30 minutes. Cool. Sprinkle with confectioners' sugar or frost with Chocolate Malt Frosting.

Chocolate Malt Frosting: Combine 1 tablespoon softened butter or margarine with 1 cup sifted confectioners' sugar, 2 tablespoons chocolate malted milk powder, ¼ teaspoon vanilla, and 1 teaspoon milk; mix well.

Satisfy even the hungriest picnicker's appetite with crispy *Sesame Chicken* and tangy *Marinated Vegetable Combo*. To avoid messy fingers, wrap the drumsticks in colorful foil.

```
┌─────────────────────────────────┐
│      AFTER-THE-GAME SUPPER      │
│                                 │
│          (14 PEOPLE)            │
│                                 │
│       Orange-Sauced Ham         │
│       Green Beans Especial      │
│  Lettuce Wedges   Chunky Dressing │
│      Hard Rolls      Butter     │
│         Chiffon Cake            │
│         Coffee      Tea         │
└─────────────────────────────────┘
```

You've invited friends over to watch the game on television, and you want to serve a simple meal afterwards. But what should you serve? Resolve your dilemma by using this menu. Prepare the salad, dessert, and crumb mixture for the beans ahead of time, then you'll need to make only an occasional trip to the kitchen to baste the ham during the game. After the game, finish preparing the vegetable and bring the food to the table. Then, call the famished sports fans to supper.

Orange-Sauced Ham

  1 5-pound canned ham
  • • •
1½ cups orange juice
⅔ cup light corn syrup
  1 tablespoon cornstarch
¾ teaspoon ground nutmeg
  1 teaspoon grated orange peel
    Orange slices
    Parsley sprigs

Place ham on rack in shallow roasting pan; mark diamond pattern on top. Bake at 325° till meat thermometer registers 140°, following timing given on label. In saucepan combine orange juice, corn syrup, cornstarch, ground nutmeg, and grated orange peel. Heat and stir till mixture boils; set aside. During last 20 minutes of baking, baste ham frequently with orange sauce. Garnish ham with orange slices and parsley. Heat remaining sauce and pass with ham. Makes 14 servings.

Green Beans Especial

Water chestnuts add crunchy texture—

  2 tablespoons butter or margarine
¾ cup soft bread crumbs
¼ cup grated Parmesan cheese
  • • •
  4 9-ounce packages frozen cut green beans
  1 8½-ounce can water chestnuts, drained and sliced
½ cup butter or margarine
  2 teaspoons lemon juice
¾ teaspoon dried basil, crushed

In small saucepan melt 2 tablespoons butter or margarine; add soft bread crumbs. Heat and stir till crumbs are golden brown. Stir in grated Parmesan cheese; set aside. Cook frozen green beans according to package directions. Drain beans; stir in sliced water chestnuts, ½ cup butter or margarine, lemon juice, and crushed basil. Cover and heat through. Turn bean mixture into warm serving dish; wreath with crumb mixture. Makes 14 servings.

Chunky Dressing

Tiny pieces of vegetables in the dressing are a pleasant surprise—

  1 cup finely chopped cucumber
¼ cup finely chopped green pepper
¼ cup thinly sliced radish
  3 tablespoons thinly sliced green onion
  2 tablespoons finely chopped canned pimiento
  • • •
1½ cups dairy sour cream
  1 cup mayonnaise or salad dressing
  2 teaspoons lemon juice
¾ teaspoon salt
⅛ teaspoon pepper

Combine chopped cucumber, green pepper, radish, green onion, and pimiento. Stir in dairy sour cream, mayonnaise or salad dressing, lemon juice, salt, and pepper; mix well. Chill thoroughly. Makes about 3 cups dressing.

```
┌─────────────────────────────┐
│      POTLUCK SUPPER (16)     │
│                             │
│  Chicken Casserole Elegante  │
│      Pear-Lime Salad         │
│  Tossed Salad     Dressing   │
│         Relishes             │
│      Rolls    Butter         │
│  Lemon Glow Angel Cake       │
│        Beverage              │
└─────────────────────────────┘
```

Want to have a party without a lot of work? Then get together with seven other couples and plan a potluck supper using the menu above. The hostess provides the beverages, and gathering place, and each of the other couples provides one part of the menu: (1) casserole (to serve 8); (2) casserole (to serve 8); (3) molded salad; (4) tossed salad and dressing; (5) rolls and butter; (6) relishes; and (7) dessert. Everyone is sure to enjoy the food and the fun of this party.

Pear-Lime Salad

    3 16-ounce cans pear slices
    3 3-ounce packages lime-flavored
      gelatin
    2 7-ounce bottles lemon-lime carbonated
      beverage, chilled
    ½ of a 6-ounce can frozen limeade
      concentrate, thawed (⅓ cup)
    2 3-ounce packages cream cheese,
      softened
    ½ cup finely chopped walnuts

Drain pears, reserving syrup; add enough water to syrup to make 2½ cups liquid. Heat reserved liquid to boiling; add gelatin and stir till dissolved. Cool. Stir in carbonated beverage and limeade concentrate. Chill till partially set. Cut cream cheese into 40 pieces. Roll each piece into ball; roll in nuts. Fold cream cheese balls and pears into gelatin. Turn into 13½x8¾x1¾-inch dish. Chill till firm. Makes 16 servings.

Chicken Casserole Elegante

    1 6-ounce package long grain and wild
      rice mix
    1 10½-ounce can condensed chicken
      broth
    1 10-ounce package frozen peas
    1 10½-ounce can condensed cream of
      mushroom soup
    ⅓ cup evaporated milk
    ⅓ cup dry sherry
    3 cups diced, cooked chicken
    1 3-ounce can sliced mushrooms,
      drained
    ¼ cup chopped canned pimiento
    1 cup soft bread crumbs
    2 tablespoons butter, melted

Cook rice mix according to package directions, *using chicken broth with enough water added* to equal liquid called for on package. Cook peas according to package directions. Combine soup and milk; stir in sherry. Add chicken, mushrooms, pimiento, rice mixture, and peas; mix well. Turn into 2-quart casserole. Cover; bake at 350° for 35 minutes. Mix crumbs and butter; sprinkle over casserole. Bake 10 minutes more. Makes 8 servings.

Lemon Glow Angel Cake

Cook one 3- or 3¼-ounce package *regular* vanilla pudding mix according to package directions. Cover surface with waxed paper; cool. Cut a 1-inch slice from top of a 10-inch angel cake; set aside. With knife parallel to cake sides, cut around cake 1 inch from center hole and 1 inch from outer edge, leaving cake walls 1 inch thick. Remove center with fork, leaving a 1-inch thick base.

Beat vanilla pudding till smooth; fold *half* the pudding into one 21-ounce can lemon pie filling. Set aside ½ *cup* of the lemon mixture; spoon remaining lemon mixture into hollow cake. Replace cake top. Prepare one 2- or 2⅛-ounce package dessert topping mix according to package directions; fold in remaining vanilla pudding. Frost cake top and sides with topping mixture; chill thoroughly. Before serving, spoon reserved lemon mixture into ring atop cake. Makes 16 servings.

```
┌──────────────────────────────┐
│      CHILDREN'S PARTY          │
│     (12 TO 14 CHILDREN)        │
│                                │
│        Drum Cake               │
│        Cherry Shakes           │
│        Candy Favors            │
└──────────────────────────────┘
```

Make your child's birthday extra special by having a costume party. Specify on the invitations that costumes are to be storybook characters—Mother Goose, Drummer Boy, Toy Soldier—made from cardboard boxes and containers appropriately decorated with paper.

After the parade of costumes, let the youngsters vote on the most original creation. A prize goes to the winner. Costumes may be set aside for other games and refreshments.

Be sure each young guest takes home a drumlike favor cup filled with candy.

Cherry Shakes

    1 3-ounce package cherry-flavored
        gelatin
    1 21-ounce can cherry pie filling
    1 quart vanilla ice cream
        Milk (about 8 cups)

Pour 1 cup boiling water and gelatin into blender container. Cover and blend till gelatin dissolves. Add pie filling. Cover and blend till smooth. Chill. At serving time, divide cherry mixture evenly between twelve to fourteen 12-ounce glasses. Add a scoop of ice cream; stir to muddle. Fill glasses with milk; stir to mix. If desired, serve with peppermint stick stirrers. Makes 12 to 14 servings.

A memorable birthday party

← At refreshment time, serve gaily decorated *Drum Cake* and *Cherry Shakes*. Fill the take-home favors with an assortment of candy.

Drum Cake

    2 cups sifted all-purpose flour
    1 cup sugar
    1 teaspoon baking soda
    1 teaspoon salt
    ½ cup shortening
    2 eggs
    1 cup buttermilk or sour milk
    2 teaspoons vanilla
    1 6-ounce package semisweet chocolate
        pieces (1 cup), melted and cooled
              • • •
    Fluffy White Frosting
    Red gumdrops
    Red licorice strings
    Black licorice sticks

Sift together first 4 ingredients into large mixer bowl. Add shortening, eggs, buttermilk, and vanilla. Blend on low speed of electric mixer, then beat on medium speed of electric mixer for 2 minutes. Combine 1 cup batter and melted chocolate. Divide light batter between two greased and floured 8x1½-inch round pans. Drop dark batter by spoonfuls on each; cut through to marble. Bake at 350° till done, 30 to 35 minutes. Cool thoroughly. Fill and frost with Fluffy White Frosting.

To decorate the cake, place small red gumdrops around bottom edge and top edge of cake; crisscross red licorice strings on sides. For drumsticks on top of cake, cross two black licorice sticks; add a large red gumdrop to the end of each licorice stick.

Fluffy White Frosting

    1 cup sugar
    ⅓ cup water
    ¼ teaspoon cream of tartar
        Dash salt
    2 egg whites
    1 teaspoon vanilla

In saucepan combine first 4 ingredients. Bring to boiling, stirring till sugar dissolves. Very slowly add sugar syrup to unbeaten egg whites in mixer bowl, beating constantly with electric mixer till stiff peaks form, about 7 minutes. Beat in vanilla. Spread on cake.

```
MAKE-A-PIZZA PARTY
(10 PEOPLE)

Pizza
Crackers and Chips   Polka-Dot Dip
Relish Tray
Ice Cream
Easy Choco Sauce   Peppermint Sauce
Soft Drinks
```

Pizza is popular with young and old alike, especially when everyone can have their favorite pizza topping. Although providing this many different pizzas may sound like a lot of work, it's not. All you do is set out a variety of toppings and let everybody make their own pizza. You can even have guests pat out the pizza crust. Just provide the balls of pizza dough and 9-inch corrugated cardboard circles covered with foil.

Pizza

> 3 cups warm water (110°)
> 3 13¾-ounce packages hot roll mix
> Salad oil
> Canned pizza sauce
> Toppings

Using the warm water and no eggs, prepare the hot roll mixes according to package directions. *Do not let rise.* Divide into 10 pieces. With oiled hands, pat each piece into an 8-inch circle on greased, foil-covered round; crimp edges. Brush each circle with salad oil. Cover with pizza sauce. Fill with desired toppings. Bake at 450° till crusts are done, about 20 minutes. Makes ten 8-inch pizzas.

Suggested Toppings: Diced Canadian bacon or ham, browned ground beef, browned sausage, sliced pepperoni, cooked shrimp, anchovies, shredded mozzarella cheese, grated Parmesan cheese, sliced mushrooms, sliced olives, chopped onion, chopped green pepper.

Polka-Dot Dip

Colorful with radish and green onion pieces —

> 2 3-ounce packages cream cheese, softened
> 1 cup dairy sour cream
> ¼ cup chopped radish
> 2 tablespoons thinly sliced green onions with tops
> ½ teaspoon dry mustard
> Milk

Combine cream cheese, sour cream, radish, onions, and mustard; add enough milk to make of dipping consistency. Chill. Serve with assorted crackers and chips. Makes 1½ cups.

Easy Choco Sauce

Starts with instant pudding —

> 1 3¾- or 3⅝-ounce package *instant* chocolate pudding
> ½ cup light corn syrup
> 1 6-ounce can evaporated milk
> 3 tablespoons milk
> ½ cup flaked coconut
> 1 teaspoon vanilla

Combine pudding mix and corn syrup; mix well. Gradually stir in evaporated milk and milk. Stir in coconut and vanilla. Chill. Serve over ice cream. Makes about 2 cups.

Peppermint Sauce

> 2 7-, 9-, or 10-ounce jars marshmallow creme
> ⅓ cup milk
> ½ cup finely crushed peppermint candy
> Red food coloring (optional)

In saucepan heat and stir marshmallow creme over low heat till softened. Blend in milk and crushed candy. Tint pink with food coloring, if desired. Stir before serving, adding additional milk if necessary to make of desired consistency. Serve warm or cool over ice cream. Makes about 2½ cups.

TEEN PARTY (14)

Super Dagwood *or* Barbecue Burgers
Potato Chips
Vegetable Relishes
Peanut Butter Bars
Soft Drinks   Iced Tea

The ingredients needed for a successful teen party are few—lots of music and lots of food. Let guests help provide the music by bringing records, and you concentrate on the food. The easiest way to serve this kind of a party is buffet-style on paper plates. This way, everybody can help themselves as often as they want and cleanup is a snap.

Super Dagwood

    2 12-inch loaves unsliced dark rye
      or white bread
  ½ cup butter or margarine
              • • •
  16 slices fully cooked ham
  12 ounces Provolone cheese (12 slices)
    1 cup Thousand Island salad dressing
      Leaf lettuce
    2 tomatoes, thinly sliced
              • • •
  14 or 16 slices cooked turkey
  16 to 20 slices salami

Cut *each* loaf bread *lengthwise* into four slices; spread with butter. *For each loaf,* place bottom slice on platter or board; top with *half* the ham and cheese. Spread with some of the salad dressing. Place second slice bread atop cheese and ham; top with lettuce, *half* the tomato, and more salad dressing. Add third slice bread; top with *half* the turkey and salami and some salad dressing. Add top slice bread. Skewer loaves from top to bottom; cut into serving-sized slices. Serves 14.

(Sandwich may be made ahead, covered with clear plastic wrap or foil, and chilled.)

Barbecue Burgers

    3 pounds ground beef
  ½ cup chopped onion
    2 10½-ounce cans condensed tomato soup
  ¾ cup water
  ⅓ cup vinegar
  ¼ cup brown sugar
    2 teaspoons chili powder
    2 teaspoons Worcestershire sauce
  ½ teaspoon celery salt
    2 bay leaves
      Hamburger buns

In Dutch oven brown the ground beef and onion; drain off excess fat. Stir in soup, water, vinegar, brown sugar, chili powder, Worcestershire sauce, celery salt, and bay leaves. Bring to boiling; reduce heat and simmer, uncovered, for 30 minutes. Serve on hamburger buns. Makes 18 to 24 sandwiches.

Peanut Butter Bars

  ½ cup shortening
  ⅔ cup chunk-style peanut butter
    1 teaspoon vanilla
    2 eggs
  1½ cups brown sugar
  1½ cups sifted all-purpose flour
  1½ teaspoons baking powder
  ½ teaspoon salt
  ¼ cup milk
    2 tablespoons butter or margarine,
      softened
  ⅓ cup chunk-style peanut butter
    2 cups sifted confectioners' sugar
      Light cream

Cream shortening, ⅔ cup peanut butter, and vanilla; beat in eggs. Mix in brown sugar. Sift together flour, baking powder, and salt. Stir into creamed mixture alternately with milk. Spread mixture in a greased 13x9x2-inch baking pan. Bake at 350° till done, about 30 minutes. (Center will be slightly soft.) Cool. For frosting, cream butter and ⅓ cup peanut butter. Slowly beat in confectioners' sugar and enough light cream to make of spreading consistency. Spread frosting over cookies. Cut in bars. Makes 18 to 24.

Recipes and Menus for Large Gatherings

Are you confronted with entertaining 18 or more guests? Don't panic! It's not as difficult as you might imagine —as long as you entertain in a style to which you are accustomed. This isn't the time to be formal if actually you enjoy more casual occasions and surroundings.

When planning the food for a large gathering, try to keep last-minute food preparation to a minimum by making as much of the food ahead as possible. Then, store the food until it is needed. Enlist some extra help, if necessary, and call on your local rental service to provide any extra equipment.

Stick with buffet-style service, whether you're hosting an open house gathering, an appetizer buffet, or a buffet supper.

Invite a large group to your holiday open house. In addition to *Minted Punch*, provide *Chewy Nut Bars*, *Sugar Cookies*, *Holiday Fruit Bread*, *Braunschweiger Pâté* with crackers, *Egg-Filled Cups*, and *Tuna Pinwheels*.

RECITES

RECIPES

(For appetizer and snack recipes see pages 98 to 103. Recipes especially suited for a large group include Prairie Fire, Ham-Cheese Logs, Salmon Boats, and Nibble Mix.)

Meat Loaf Trio

3 beaten eggs
1½ cups milk
3 cups soft bread crumbs
1 cup chopped onion
½ cup chopped green pepper
5 pounds ground beef
1 pound ground pork
¾ cup catsup
¼ cup brown sugar
1 tablespoon dry mustard

Combine first 5 ingredients, 1 tablespoon salt, and ¼ teaspoon pepper. Add meats; mix. Shape into three 7½x4-inch loaves; square off ends. Place in a 15½x10½x1-inch baking pan. Bake at 350° for 1 hour. Spoon off excess fat. Combine remaining ingredients. Spread over loaves. Bake 15 minutes more. Serves 24.

Chicken Barbecue

6 ready-to-cook broiler-fryer
chickens, quartered
Salad oil
2 cups catsup
½ cup finely chopped onion
½ cup butter, melted
½ cup molasses
¼ cup vinegar

Brush chicken quarters with salad oil. Season with salt and pepper. Place chicken, bone side down, on grill. Grill over slow coals 20 to 30 minutes. Turn; grill till done, 20 to 30 minutes more, turning occasionally. During last 15 minutes of grilling, brush occasionally with a mixture of the remaining ingredients. Makes 24 servings.

Pear-Sauced Pork Roasts

2 9-pound boneless pork loin roasts
4 teaspoons ground ginger
1 teaspoon pepper
2 29-ounce cans pears
1 cup dry white wine
¼ cup cornstarch
2 cups seedless grapes, halved

Rub roasts with a mixture of *3 teaspoons* ginger, 2 teaspoons salt, and pepper. Place on racks in shallow roasting pan. Roast, uncovered, at 325° till meat thermometer registers 170°, about 3½ to 4 hours. Drain pears, reserving syrup. Cut up pears. In a saucepan blend wine and cornstarch. Add reserved pear syrup, pear pieces, 1 teaspoon ginger, and ¼ teaspoon salt. Cook and stir till thickened and bubbly. Cook 1 minute longer. Add grapes; heat. Spoon some of the sauce over roasts; pass remaining. Makes 24 to 30 servings.

Fruited Turkey Roasts

2 3-pound frozen boneless turkey
roasts
1 16-ounce can crushed pineapple
2 10-ounce jars cherry preserves
¼ cup lemon juice
1 teaspoon ground cinnamon

Prepare turkey roasts, following package directions. Drain pineapple. In saucepan combine pineapple, cherry preserves, lemon juice, and cinnamon; heat. Before serving, spoon some of the hot pineapple mixture over turkey. Pass remaining sauce. Serves 22.

Turkey that's easy to serve

When you're challenged with cooking for a crowd, take advantage of convenience products and prepare *Fruited Turkey Roasts.*

84

Barbecue-Glazed Ham

1 10-pound fully cooked, formed ham
1 4½-ounce jar strained apricots
  (baby food)
¼ cup brown sugar
3 tablespoons chili sauce
1 tablespoon vinegar
⅛ teaspoon ground cloves

Have meatman slice ham in serving-sized pieces and tie together in original shape. Place ham on rack in shallow roasting pan. Do not cover or add water. Bake at 325° about 2 hours. Combine strained apricots, brown sugar, chili sauce, vinegar, and cloves. Brush over ham and continue roasting 30 minutes longer, brushing occasionally with apricot mixture. Transfer ham to serving platter and untie. Makes 20 to 30 servings.

Shellfish Newburg

3 pounds fresh or frozen shrimp in
  shells
6 10½-ounce cans condensed cream of
  mushroom soup
2 cups light cream
6 beaten egg yolks
1 cup dry white wine
2 tablespoons lemon juice
1 16-ounce package frozen crab meat,
  thawed, flaked, and cartilage
  removed
  Patty shells or toast points
  Snipped parsley

In large saucepan bring 2 quarts water and 3 tablespoons salt to boiling. Add shrimp. Heat to boiling; reduce heat and simmer till shrimp turn pink, 1 to 3 minutes. Drain. Peel shrimp and remove black vein. Split peeled shrimp lengthwise.

In large Dutch oven blend soup and cream. Heat just to boiling, stirring occasionally. Stir a moderate amount of hot sauce into egg yolks. Return to sauce. Stir over low heat till thickened. Stir in wine, lemon juice, shrimp, and crab. Heat through. Serve sauce in patty shells or over toast points. Garnish with parsley. Makes 20 to 25 servings.

Stroganoff for a Crowd

8 pounds beef round steak, ½ inch
  thick
¼ cup shortening
¼ teaspoon pepper
2 cups chopped onion
2 cloves garlic, minced
2 6-ounce cans sliced mushrooms
4 10½-ounce cans condensed cream
  of mushroom soup
1 10½-ounce can condensed beef broth
1 6-ounce can tomato paste
3 cups dairy sour cream
18 ounces noodles

Partially freeze meat for easier cutting. Cut meat into 2x½-inch strips. In large kettle or Dutch oven brown the meat, one pound at a time, in hot shortening. Return all meat to kettle; sprinkle with pepper. Add onion, garlic, and mushrooms. Combine soup, beef broth, and tomato paste; blend till smooth. Add to meat. Cover; simmer till meat is tender, about 1¼ hours, stirring occasionally. Stir some of the hot mixture into sour cream; return to meat mixture and heat through (*do not boil*). Cook noodles in large amount of boiling, salted water according to package directions. Serve meat over hot noodles. Serves 24.

Pineapple-Berry Freeze

2 14-ounce jars cranberry-orange
  relish
1 13½-ounce can crushed pineapple
1 10½-ounce package miniature
  marshmallows
1 cup chopped pecans
¼ cup mayonnaise or salad dressing
2 cups whipping cream
  Lettuce

In large bowl combine relish, undrained pineapple, marshmallows, pecans, and mayonnaise. Whip cream; fold into fruit mixture. Tint pink with red food coloring, if desired. Turn into two 9x5x3-inch loaf pans. Freeze till firm. Let stand at room temperature 10 minutes before unmolding. Slice; serve on lettuce-lined plates. Makes 20 to 24 servings.

Scalloped Succotash Bake

Cut the recipe in half to make 12 servings—

    4 17-ounce cans whole kernel corn,
        drained
    2 16-ounce cans green lima beans,
        drained
    2 14½-ounce cans evaporated milk
    4 beaten eggs
    12 ounces process Swiss cheese,
        shredded (3 cups)
    ½ cup sliced green onion
    ½ cup chopped canned pimiento
    1½ teaspoons salt
    ⅛ teaspoon pepper
    4 cups soft bread crumbs
    3 tablespoons butter, melted

Combine corn, limas, evaporated milk, eggs, cheese, onion, pimiento, salt, and pepper. Turn into two 13½x8¾x1¾-inch baking dishes. Toss together the crumbs and butter. Sprinkle *half* of the crumbs atop *each* casserole. Bake at 350° about 40 minutes. Let stand 5 minutes before serving. Makes 24 servings.

Greens and Beans Salad

    2 cups salad oil
    ½ cup vinegar
    1 tablespoon sugar
    1 teaspoon celery seed
    1 teaspoon paprika
    4 16-ounce cans cut green beans,
        drained
    16 cups torn lettuce, chilled
    8 cups torn fresh spinach, chilled
    8 ounces natural Swiss cheese,
        shredded (2 cups)

In large jar with tight-fitting lid, combine first 5 ingredients and 2 teaspoons salt; cover and shake to mix. Pour over beans; marinate in refrigerator at least 2 hours. Just before serving, drain beans, reserving marinade. In several large salad bowls or a large plastic bag toss beans with lettuce, spinach, and cheese. Add enough of reserved marinade to thoroughly coat greens. Serve in large salad bowls. Makes about 30 servings.

Party Potato Salad

Soak 4 teaspoons mustard seed and 1 tablespoon celery seed in ⅓ cup vinegar for several hours or overnight. Cook, peel, and cube 6 pounds potatoes (about 15 cups). Sprinkle potatoes with salt. Toss potatoes with 2 cups chopped celery; 1 cup finely chopped green onion and tops; and 6 hard-cooked eggs, chopped. Combine 4 cups mayonnaise, seed mixture, and 2 teaspoons salt. Add mayonnaise mixture to potato mixture; toss to mix. For thorough chilling, refrigerate salad in 2 large bowls. Garnish with hard-cooked egg wedges. Makes 24 to 30 servings.

Croissants

These are extra good served warm—

Cream 1½ cups butter and ⅓ cup sifted all-purpose flour. Roll between waxed paper to 12x6-inch rectangle. Chill at least 1 hour.

Soften 2 packages active dry yeast in ½ cup *warm* water. Scald ¾ cup milk. Add ¼ cup sugar and 1 teaspoon salt to milk; cool to lukewarm. Add yeast and 1 beaten egg; mix well. Using 3¾ to 4 cups sifted all-purpose flour, add enough of the flour to make a soft dough. Knead on floured surface 5 minutes. Roll to 14-inch square. Place *chilled* butter on one half; fold over other half and seal. Roll to a 20x12-inch rectangle; seal.

Fold dough in thirds. (If butter softens, chill after each rolling.) Roll to a 20x12-inch rectangle. Fold in thirds and roll twice more; seal edges. Fold in thirds to a 12x7-inch rectangle. Chill 45 minutes. Cut dough crosswise in fourths. Roll one-fourth of dough (keep remainder chilled) to paper-thin 22x7-inch rectangle. Cut in 10 pie-shaped wedges, 4 inches at base and 7 inches long (put together extra ½ wedge from each end). To shape each roll, begin with base of wedge and roll loosely toward point. Repeat with remaining three-fourths of the dough.

Place rolls, 3 inches apart, on ungreased baking sheet, point down; curve. Cover; let double, 30 to 45 minutes. Beat 1 egg yolk with 1 tablespoon milk; brush on rolls. Bake at 375° for 12 to 15 minutes. Makes 40.

Strawberry-Nut Bread

Small loaves are easy to slice and serve—

    1 cup butter or margarine
1½ cups sugar
    1 teaspoon vanilla
    ¼ teaspoon lemon extract
    4 eggs
         • • •
    3 cups sifted all-purpose flour
    1 teaspoon salt
    1 teaspoon cream of tartar
    ½ teaspoon baking soda
         • • •
    1 cup strawberry jam
    ½ cup dairy sour cream
    1 cup broken walnuts

In mixing bowl cream together butter or margarine, sugar, vanilla, and lemon extract till fluffy. Add eggs, one at a time, beating well after each addition. Sift together flour, salt, cream of tartar, and baking soda. Combine jam and sour cream. Add jam mixture alternately with dry ingredients to creamed mixture, beating till well combined. Stir in walnuts. Divide among five greased and floured 4½x 2¾x2¼-inch loaf pans. Bake at 350° till done, about 50 to 55 minutes. Cool 10 minutes in pans; remove and cool completely on wire racks. Makes 5 loaves.

Melon Medley

    ½ watermelon, cut lengthwise
    2 cantaloupes, peeled and seeded
    1 honeydew, peeled and seeded
    1 ⁴/₅-quart bottle rosé wine
    2 quarts raspberry sherbet

Scoop pulp from watermelon, using a melon ball cutter; discard seeds and juice from watermelon. Leave shell intact; scallop edges, if desired. Cut cantaloupe into small chunks. Cut honeydew in thin slices. Combine watermelon balls, cantaloupe, and honeydew; return to watermelon shell. Pour rosé wine over fruit. Refrigerate several hours to thoroughly chill. Serve fruit mixture over scoops of raspberry sherbet. Makes 20 servings.

Petits Fours

    ¼ cup butter or margarine
    ¼ cup shortening
1¼ cups sugar
    ½ teaspoon vanilla
    ¼ teaspoon almond extract
    2 cups sifted cake flour
    3 teaspoons baking powder
    ¾ cup milk
    ¾ cup egg whites (6)
    Petits Fours Icing
    Decorations

Cream first 2 ingredients. Gradually add *1 cup* sugar, creaming till light. Stir in vanilla and almond extract. Sift together flour, baking powder, and ¼ teaspoon salt; add to creamed mixture alternately with milk, beating well after each addition. Beat whites till foamy; gradually add remaining sugar, beating till soft peaks form. Fold into batter. Turn into greased and lightly floured 13x9x2-inch baking pan. Bake at 350° about 40 minutes. Cool 10 minutes; remove from pan. Cool.

Cut cooled cake in 1½-inch diamonds, squares, or circles, using a stiff paper pattern. Place cakes on rack with cookie sheet below. Spoon Petits Fours Icing over cakes. Let dry; add another coat. Decorate with sliced almonds, marshmallows or fruit slice flowers, or flowers made with Ornamental Frosting.

Petits Fours Icing: In covered 2-quart saucepan bring 3 cups granulated sugar, ¼ teaspoon cream of tartar, and 1½ cups hot water to boiling. Uncover; continue cooking to thin syrup (226°). Cool at room temperature, not over ice water, to lukewarm (110°). Add 1 teaspoon vanilla and enough sifted confectioners' sugar (about 2½ cups) to make of pouring consistency. Tint with food coloring, if desired.

Ornamental Frosting: With electric mixer blend 1 cup shortening and 1 teaspoon vanilla. Slowly add 4 cups sifted confectioners' sugar; beat just till combined. Stir in about 1½ tablespoons milk. Make trial flower to check frosting consistency. If frosting is too stiff, add a few drops more milk. Tint to desired color. Make flowers with pastry tube on silicone paper or waxed paper. Place on cookie sheet. Harden in refrigerator or freezer 1 hour. Transfer to cake with spatula.

Chocolate Revel Bars

     1 cup butter or margarine
     2 cups brown sugar
     2 eggs
     2 teaspoons vanilla
  2½ cups sifted all-purpose flour
     1 teaspoon baking soda
     3 cups quick-cooking rolled oats
     1 15-ounce can *sweetened condensed*
        milk
     1 12-ounce package semisweet chocolate
        pieces (2 cups)
     2 tablespoons butter or margarine
     1 cup chopped walnuts
     2 teaspoons vanilla

In large bowl cream 1 cup butter and brown sugar. Beat in eggs and 2 teaspoons vanilla. Sift together flour, soda, and 1 teaspoon salt; stir in oats. Stir dry ingredients into creamed mixture till blended; set aside. In heavy saucepan heat together sweetened condensed milk, chocolate, 2 tablespoons butter, and ½ teaspoon salt over low heat, stirring till smooth. Stir in nuts and 2 teaspoons vanilla. Pat ⅔ of oat mixture in bottom of 15½x10½x1-inch baking pan. Spread chocolate mixture over dough. Dot with remaining oat mixture. Bake at 350° for 25 to 30 minutes; cool. Cut in 2x1-inch bars. Makes 75.

Fruited Layer Squares

Sift together 1½ cups sifted all-purpose flour, 1 tablespoon sugar, and ½ teaspoon salt. Cut in 6 tablespoons butter till mixture resembles coarse crumbs. Combine 2 egg yolks, ¼ cup dairy sour cream, and ½ teaspoon vanilla; stir into flour mixture. Pat into greased 13x9x2-inch baking pan. Bake at 350° for 20 minutes. Combine 1 cup finely snipped dates, ¾ cup dairy sour cream, ⅓ cup apricot preserves, and 2 teaspoons grated orange peel; spread over baked layer. Beat 2 egg whites to soft peaks. Gradually add 7 tablespoons sugar and ½ teaspoon ground cinnamon; beat to stiff peaks. Carefully spread meringue atop date mixture; sprinkle with ⅓ cup chopped walnuts. Bake at 350° till browned, 30 minutes. Cool; cut in squares. Makes 48.

Strawberry Delight

Next time, use frozen raspberries and raspberry-flavored gelatin —

     1 11¼-ounce frozen loaf pound cake,
        thawed
     3 3-ounce packages strawberry-
        flavored gelatin
     3 cups boiling water
     2 16-ounce packages frozen sliced
        strawberries
     2 cups whipping cream

Cut pound cake crosswise into 16 thin slices. Fit cake slices into the bottoms of two 9x9x2-inch baking pans. In large bowl dissolve strawberry-flavored gelatin in the boiling water. Add frozen strawberries and let stand till berries are thawed and gelatin thickens slightly. Stir occasionally. Whip cream just till soft peaks form. Fold into partially set gelatin mixture. If necessary, chill till mixture mounds. Pour *half* the strawberry mixture over pound cake in *each* pan. Chill several hours or overnight. To serve, cut into squares. Makes 18 servings.

Chocolate Surprise

     1 12-ounce package semisweet chocolate
        pieces (2 cups)
     2 tablespoons sugar
     3 beaten egg yolks
     3 stiffly beaten egg whites
               • • •
     2 cups whipping cream
     1 small angel food cake, cut in bite-
        sized pieces (10 cups)
     ½ cup toasted chopped almonds

In top of double boiler, melt chocolate pieces. Add sugar and stir till melted. Blend in beaten egg yolks; mix well. Remove from heat. Fold in beaten egg whites. Set aside to cool. Whip cream. Fold into chocolate mixture. Pour chocolate mixture over cake pieces; fold together carefully. Spread in a 13½x8¾x1¾-inch baking dish. Sprinkle almonds on top. Chill several hours. To serve, cut into squares. Makes 18 servings.

MENUS

```
┌──────────────────────────────┐
       HOLIDAY PARTY (30)

  Braunschweiger Pâté    Crackers
  Tuna Pinwheels    Egg-Filled Cups
  Chewy Nut Bars    Sugar Cookies
        Holiday Fruit Bread
           Minted Punch
└──────────────────────────────┘
```

When holiday time arrives, hold a festive open house for your friends. Create the appropriate joyous mood with colorful decorations and cheerful background music.

Since this party will span several hours, serve the food from a buffet table replenished frequently from the kitchen.

Sugar Cookies

As shown at the beginning of this section—

    1 cup butter or margarine
    1 cup sugar
    1 beaten egg
    1 teaspoon vanilla
    2 cups sifted all-purpose flour
    ½ teaspoon baking soda
    ½ teaspoon cream of tartar
      Red and green colored sugar

Cream butter and 1 cup sugar till fluffy. Mix in egg and vanilla. Sift together flour, soda, cream of tartar, and ¼ teaspoon salt. Blend into creamed mixture; mix well. Shape dough into small balls about the size of a nickle. Place on ungreased cookie sheet. Dip bottom of small glass in colored sugar (to get sugar to stick, first press bottom of glass in cookie dough); use glass to flatten cookies. Bake at 375° till lightly browned, 8 to 10 minutes. Makes about 60 cookies.

Chewy Nut Bars

Line bottom and sides of 13x9x2-inch baking pan with foil. Melt ¼ cup butter in pan. Sift together ⅔ cup sifted all-purpose flour, ¼ teaspoon baking soda, and ¼ teaspoon salt. Stir in 2 cups brown sugar and 2 cups finely chopped nuts. Blend in 4 beaten eggs and 2 teaspoons vanilla. *Carefully* spoon batter over butter in pan. *Don't stir.* Bake at 350° about 25 minutes. Don't overbake. Dust with confectioners' sugar. Place waxed paper under wire racks. Immediately invert pan onto racks to remove cookies; peel off foil. Cool. Dust with confectioners' sugar. Cut into 36 bars.

Egg-Filled Cups

Combine 4 hard-cooked eggs, chopped; 2 tablespoons *each* chopped radish and mayonnaise; 1 tablespoon *each* chopped green onion and Italian salad dressing; and ¼ teaspoon *each* Worcestershire sauce and salt. Chill. Cut 1 loaf unsliced whole wheat bread into 1-inch thick slices. Cut slices into rounds with small cutter. Hollow out rounds with kitchen shears, leaving about ¼ inch on sides and bottoms. Brush inside of bread cups with mayonnaise; fill with 2 tablespoons egg mixture. Trim with radish and parsley. Makes 30.

Holiday Fruit Bread

Cream ½ cup butter and 1 cup sugar. Blend in 2 large bananas, mashed; 2 beaten eggs; and 1 teaspoon vanilla. Sift together 2 cups sifted all-purpose flour and 1 teaspoon baking soda. Blend into creamed mixture. Mix in ½ cup semisweet chocolate pieces, ⅓ cup chopped maraschino cherries, and ¼ cup chopped nuts. Fill 5 well-greased and floured 10½-ounce soup cans *half* full of batter. Bake at 350° till done, about 40 minutes. Remove from cans; cool thoroughly. Wrap in foil; refrigerate till used. Slice to serve. Makes 5 loaves.

Tuna Pinwheels

Dainty party sandwiches —

  1 loaf unsliced white bread
  ⅓ cup butter or margarine, softened
  2 6½- or 7-ounce cans tuna, drained
     and flaked
  ⅔ cup mayonnaise or salad dressing
  2 tablespoons mashed canned pimiento
  1 tablespoon prepared mustard
       • • •
  40 very thin strips green pepper

Have bakery cut bread into 8 *lengthwise* slices about ¼ inch thick. Trim crusts. Roll bread lightly with a rolling pin. Spread bread with softened butter or margarine. Combine tuna, mayonnaise or salad dressing, pimiento, and mustard. Spread each slice of bread with about ¼ cup filling. Place 5 strips green pepper, equal distance apart, atop filling on each bread slice. Roll up jelly-roll style, beginning at narrow end. Wrap in foil or clear plastic wrap; chill. Slice into ⅜-inch pinwheels. Makes 40 sandwiches.

To make *Egg-Filled Cups,* snip out the center of bread rounds to form cups. Then, fill with egg salad mixture and garnish with radishes.

Braunschweiger Pâté

In mixer bowl combine 1 pound braunschweiger, broken up; *half* of an 8-ounce package cream cheese, softened; 1 tablespoon *each* milk and grated onion; and 1 teaspoon *each* sugar and chili powder. Beat smooth. Form into an igloo shape; place on plate. Cover; chill. Whip remaining *half* package cream cheese, 1 tablespoon milk, and ⅛ teaspoon bottled hot pepper sauce till smooth. Spread evenly over braunschweiger; chill. Garnish with snipped parsley. Serve with crackers.

Minted Punch

In saucepan mix three 10-ounce jars mint-flavored apple jelly and 4 cups water. Heat and stir till jelly melts. Mix 3 cups sugar and 6 packages unsweetened lemonade-flavored soft drink powder; stir into jelly. Add 8 cups pineapple juice. Chill. Pour chilled mixture over ice in punch bowl. Add four 28-ounce bottles lemon-lime carbonated beverage, chilled. Makes about 55 (4-ounce) servings.

For *Tuna Pinwheels,* spread bread with filling and place green pepper strips atop. Carefully roll up as shown. Chill, then slice.

BUFFET SUPPER (24)

Curried Ham   Condiments
Oven Rice
Marinated Bean Salad
French Bread   Butter
Fresh Fruit Plate
Coffee   Irish Coffee

Having a crowd over for supper? Then, treat them to this tasty, yet simple meal. Place all the food, including the fresh fruit dessert, on a buffet table and let guests serve themselves. After the meal, offer your guests a choice of a second cup of hot coffee or a cup of whiskey-laced Irish Coffee.

Curried Ham

1½ cups chopped onion
6 tablespoons butter or margarine
• • •
¼ cup all-purpose flour
2 tablespoons curry powder
2 10½-ounce cans condensed cream of
    mushroom soup
5 cups milk
12 cups cubed fully cooked ham
4 cups dairy sour cream
• • •
Toasted slivered almonds
Snipped parsley
Condiments

In large Dutch oven cook onion in butter till tender but not brown. Blend in flour and curry powder. Add soup. Gradually stir in milk; cook and stir till thickened and bubbly. Add ham and heat through. Add sour cream; cook and stir till heated through (*do not boil*). Garnish with toasted slivered almonds and snipped parsley, if desired. Serve with Oven Rice and Condiments. Serves 24.

Condiments: Chutney, sliced green onion, sliced preserved kumquats, and flaked coconut.

Oven Rice

Place 2 cups long grain rice in *each* of two 2-quart casseroles. Add 2 teaspoons salt and 5 cups water to *each* casserole. Cover; bake at 350° for 30 minutes. Fluff with fork. Cover; continue baking till tender, 20 to 30 minutes more. Makes 24 servings.

Marinated Bean Salad

Boiling water
4 9-ounce packages frozen French-
    style green beans, thawed
2 large onions, thinly sliced and
    separated into rings
2 6-ounce cans sliced mushrooms,
    drained
1⅓ cups Italian salad dressing
Romaine
6 medium tomatoes

Pour boiling water over beans; let stand 5 minutes. Drain thoroughly. Combine beans, onion rings, and mushrooms; add salad dressing, 1 teaspoon salt, and ¼ teaspoon pepper. Toss together. Marinate in refrigerator several hours or overnight, tossing occasionally. At serving time, spoon bean mixture into serving bowl lined with romaine. Cut tomatoes into wedges and arrange them decoratively around the edge of the bowl. Makes 24 servings.

Irish Coffee

For each serving pour 1 jigger Irish whiskey (1½ ounces) into a glass or mug. (Plan to get 16 servings per ⅘-quart bottle of whiskey.) Add 1 to 2 teaspoons sugar to each glass; stir to dissolve sugar. Fill glass with very hot, strong coffee. Top with a dollop of unsweetened whipped cream.

Buffet for a crowd

Accompany *Curried Ham* and *Oven Rice*, → placed on a warming tray, with *Marinated Bean Salad*, French bread, and fresh fruit.

```
  ┌─────────────────────────────────┐
        APPETIZER BUFFET (20)

   Sweet-Sour Franks    Tomato Tidbits
    Smoky Cheese Ball    Crackers
    Shrimp Dip    Vegetable Dippers
       Lemon-Apple Sparkle
  └─────────────────────────────────┘
```

Want to have a party without preparing a full meal? If so, feed your guests the easy way by serving the appealing assortment of appetizers shown on the cover.

Plan the party around an activity such as table games or cards. Then, set up the buffet table in a handy spot so that guests can help themselves to the food whenever there is a break in their game.

Sweet-Sour Franks

      3 tablespoons cornstarch
   ⅓ cup sugar
   1 cup pineapple juice
   1 8-ounce can tomato sauce
   ⅓ cup vinegar
   4 5-ounce packages cocktail
        frankfurters (64)

In blazer pan of chafing dish, combine cornstarch and sugar; blend in pineapple juice. Stir in tomato sauce and vinegar. Cook and stir over direct heat till thickened and bubbly. Cover; simmer for 5 minutes. Add frankfurters; heat through. Keep warm over hot water (bain-marie). Makes 64.

Smoky Cheese Ball

Combine two 8-ounce packages cream cheese, softened; 8 ounces smoky Cheddar cheese, shredded (2 cups); ½ cup butter or margarine, softened; 2 tablespoons milk; and 2 teaspoons steak sauce. Beat till fluffy. Chill slightly. Shape into ball; coat with 1 cup finely chopped toasted almonds. Serve with crackers.

Tomato Tidbits

Mix 1 cup finely chopped cooked chicken; ¼ cup finely chopped celery; 1 tablespoon finely chopped onion; 1 tablespoon pickle relish, well drained; and ¼ teaspoon *each* curry powder and salt. Moisten with ¼ cup mayonnaise. Chill. Cut small portion off bottoms of 40 cherry tomatoes so they will sit flat. Cut thin slice from tops of tomatoes; with small melon baller or spoon carefully scoop out centers and discard. Sprinkle insides with salt and pepper. Invert; chill. Fill tomatoes with chicken mixture, using 1 to 1½ teaspoons for each tomato. Makes 40.

Shrimp Dip

Combine one 4½-ounce can shrimp, drained and finely chopped; 1 hard-cooked egg, chopped; 1 cup dairy sour cream; ¼ cup mayonnaise; 3 tablespoons thinly sliced green onion with tops; 1 tablespoon lemon juice; 1 teaspoon prepared horseradish; 1 teaspoon Worcestershire sauce; and ½ teaspoon dried dillweed, crushed. Mix well. Cover; chill. Serve with crisp vegetable dippers. Makes about 2 cups.

Lemon-Apple Sparkle

   12 cups apple juice
    8 inches stick cinnamon
   24 whole cloves
    3 whole allspice
    4 6-ounce cans frozen lemonade
        concentrate
      Ice cubes
    2 28-ounce bottles ginger ale,
        chilled
      Yellow food coloring
      Lemon slices

In saucepan combine *3 cups* apple juice and the spices. Simmer, covered, for 15 minutes; strain. Stir in concentrate till melted. Add remaining apple juice. Chill. At serving time, pour lemonade mixture over ice in punch bowl. Slowly add ginger ale. Tint with food coloring, if desired. Garnish with lemon slices. Makes about 35 (5-ounce) servings.

```
┌─────────────────────────────┐
│                             │
│   MAKE-AHEAD SHOWER (18)    │
│                             │
│   Party Sandwich Loaves     │
│     Mints    Nuts           │
│    Elegant Fruit Punch      │
│           or                │
│      Four-Fruit Punch       │
│                             │
└─────────────────────────────┘
```

Are you hostessing a bridal shower or a baby shower? No need to worry about refreshments. Just serve the delicious foods in this menu. And, since most of the food preparation can be done several hours ahead, you'll have plenty of time for last-minute decorating.

Elegant Fruit Punch

    2 cups cranberry juice cocktail
    1 6-ounce can frozen orange juice
        concentrate, thawed
    1 6-ounce can frozen lemonade
        concentrate, thawed
    ½ cup sugar
    2 25-ounce bottles sparkling pink
        catawba juice, chilled

Advance preparation: In large bowl combine cranberry juice, concentrates, and 3 cups water. Stir to blend. Add sugar; stir till dissolved. Chill thoroughly.

Before serving: Slowly add catawba juice; blend. Makes 24 (4-ounce) servings.

Four-Fruit Punch

Advance preparation: In large bowl combine 3 cups apricot nectar; 2 cups pineapple juice; one 6-ounce can frozen orange juice concentrate, thawed; ½ cup lemon juice; and ¼ cup sugar. Stir to dissolve sugar. Chill.

Before serving: Slowly add one 32-ounce bottle ginger ale, chilled; mix till blended. Add 1 pint pineapple sherbet in scoopfuls. Makes 24 (4-ounce) servings.

Party Sandwich Loaves

    1 loaf unsliced white bread
    1 loaf unsliced whole wheat bread
        Butter or margarine, softened
        Chicken Salad Filling
    2 5-ounce jars process cheese spread
        with pimiento
        Egg Salad Filling
    3 8-ounce packages cream cheese,
        softened
    ⅓ cup milk
        Snipped parsley

Advance preparation: Remove crusts from bread. Slice *each* loaf *lengthwise* into 4 layers. Spread layers with butter. Spread first layer of *each* loaf with *half* the Chicken Salad Filling. Spread *half* the cheese spread on second layer of *each* loaf. Spread *half* the Egg Salad Filling on third layer of *each* loaf. Assemble loaves, alternating white and whole wheat layers. Place fourth bread layer on top. Beat cream cheese with milk till fluffy. Frost top and sides of loaves. Cover sandwich loaves loosely with clear plastic wrap propped up with wooden picks. Chill a few hours.

Before serving: Using 2 spatulas, transfer to serving plates. Trim with parsley. Serves 18.

Chicken Salad Filling

    2 cups ground cooked chicken
    ½ cup finely chopped celery
    ¼ cup finely chopped green pepper
    ¾ cup mayonnaise or salad dressing

In bowl combine all ingredients and ¼ teaspoon salt; mix well. Makes 2½ cups.

Egg Salad Filling

    6 hard-cooked eggs, finely chopped
    ⅓ cup finely chopped dill pickle
    1 tablespoon finely sliced green
        onion
    ½ cup mayonnaise or salad dressing

In bowl combine all ingredients and ¼ teaspoon salt; mix well. Makes about 2 cups.

Appetizers, Snacks, and Beverages

When you don't want to serve a complete meal, try between-meal entertaining that requires only appetizers and snacks. These kinds of foods are suitable for groups of all sizes. The larger the group, the greater the variety and quantity. When entertaining a smaller group, you might choose two or three appetizers or snacks. Then, as the party size increases, add extra foods and increase the quantity of food. Be sure to have enough of each item so that guests can sample some of everything.

To accompany the food, choose from the assortment of punches, beverages, or cocktails on the following pages. If you're a bit unsure how to stock your bar or serve wines and after-dinner drinks, check the information on pages 109-111.

Choose from this tempting assortment of appetizers and beverages when entertaining at between-meal parties. Included are *Nibble Mix, Peach Spike, Hot Malted-Mint Drink, Raspberry Punch,* hot *Mock Quiche Squares,* and elegant *Caviar Log.*

APPETIZERS AND SNACKS

Fruit Kabobs

Subtly ginger-flavored—

1 13½-ounce can pineapple chunks
¼ cup orange marmalade
¾ teaspoon ground ginger

• • •

1 11-ounce can mandarin orange
   sections, drained
1 cup maraschino cherries, well
   drained
1 cup honeydew balls
2 large oranges
2 small bananas

Drain pineapple, reserving syrup. Combine reserved syrup, marmalade, and ginger. Add pineapple, mandarin oranges, cherries, and honeydew. Chill. Drain well, reserving marinade. Cut thin slice off bottom of oranges so they will sit level. Slice bananas; dip in reserved marinade. Skewer pieces of fruit on long wooden picks. To serve, anchor twelve of the kabobs in each orange. Makes 24.

Nibble Mix

As shown at the beginning of this section—

6 cups bite-sized shredded corn
   squares
3 cups pretzel sticks
1 3-ounce can chow mein noodles
½ cup butter or margarine, melted
¾ cup grated Parmesan cheese
1 tablespoon garlic salad dressing
   mix

In 13x9x2-inch baking pan heat corn squares, pretzel sticks, and chow mein noodles at 300° till warm, about 5 minutes. Remove from oven. Pour the melted butter over mixture; sprinkle with cheese and dry salad dressing mix. Stir well. Return to oven and heat 15 to 20 minutes more. Makes about 12 cups.

Stuffed Eggs

8 hard-cooked eggs, peeled
3 tablespoons creamy Italian salad
   dressing
1 tablespoon milk
   Dash Worcestershire sauce

Cut eggs in half lengthwise, using a zigzag cut or a crinkle cutter. Remove yolks. Combine yolks, salad dressing, milk, Worcestershire, and dash pepper. Pipe egg yolk mixture into egg whites. Chill. Makes 16.

Dill-Sour Cream Dip

1 cup dairy sour cream
½ cup mayonnaise or salad dressing
1 tablespoon finely chopped green
   onion
2 teaspoons dried parsley flakes,
   crushed
1 teaspoon dried dillweed
1 teaspoon seasoned salt
   Crackers or vegetable dippers

Combine first 6 ingredients. Cover and chill several hours. Serve with crackers or vegetable dippers. Makes about 1½ cups.

Smoked Oyster Dip

1 3-ounce package cream cheese,
   softened
2 tablespoons mayonnaise
2 tablespoons milk
1 tablespoon finely chopped onion
2 teaspoons chopped canned pimiento
1 3⅔-ounce can smoked oysters,
   drained and chopped
   Assorted crackers or chips

Combine cream cheese, mayonnaise, milk, onion, pimiento, and oysters; mix well. Chill. Serve with crackers or chips. Makes 1 cup.

Prairie Fire

For a smaller party, cut the recipe in half—

    4 16-ounce cans red kidney beans
    ½ cup butter or margarine
    8 ounces Provolone cheese, shredded
       (2 cups)
    ¼ to ⅓ cup finely chopped hot peppers
    2 tablespoons minced onion
    2 cloves garlic, minced
      Corn chips or tortilla chips

Drain beans, reserving ⅔ cup liquid; mash. In saucepan combine beans, reserved liquid, butter, cheese, peppers, onion, garlic, and ½ teaspoon salt. Heat and stir till hot. Transfer to chafing dish; place over hot water (bain-marie). Serve with chips. Makes 6 cups.

Hot Cheese-Chive Dip

    1 8-ounce package cream cheese,
      softened
    4 ounces sharp process American
      cheese, shredded (1 cup)
    ¼ cup dry white wine
    2 tablespoons milk
    1 tablespoon snipped chives
    ¼ teaspoon dry mustard
      Shredded wheat wafers

In saucepan heat and stir softened cream cheese and shredded American cheese over low heat till blended. Stir in dry white wine, milk, chives, and dry mustard. Pour into small chafing dish, adding more milk if mixture becomes too thick. Serve with shredded wheat wafers. Makes 1⅔ cups.

Looking for a good appetizer or snack recipe? Choose from a variety including *Notches* (page 102), *Hot Cheese-Chive Dip, Stuffed Eggs, Tiny Ham Puffs* (page 101), and *Fruit Kabobs.*

Yogurt-Cuke Dip

    1 cup plain yogurt
    ½ teaspoon dried dillweed
    ½ teaspoon onion salt
    ½ teaspoon dried parsley flakes
    2 cucumbers, peeled and cut in sticks

Combine first 4 ingredients; chill. Stand cucumber sticks around edge of small, deep bowl. Fill with yogurt mixture. Makes 1 cup.

Creamy Blue Cheese Dip

    1 cup dairy sour cream
    ¼ cup mayonnaise or salad dressing
    2 ounces blue cheese, crumbled
        (½ cup)
    1 tablespoon milk
    1 teaspoon lemon juice
    Vegetable dippers

Blend sour cream, mayonnaise, and *half* the blue cheese. Add milk and lemon juice; beat smooth with rotary beater. Chill. Garnish with remaining blue cheese. Serve with vegetable dippers. Makes about 1⅓ cups.

Accompany *Creamy Blue Cheese Dip* with crisp celery sticks, bright red cherry tomatoes, crinkle-cut carrots, and cucumber sticks.

Avocado-Beef Spread

    1 4½-ounce can corned beef spread
        or deviled ham
    2 avocados, peeled and mashed
    1 tablespoon finely chopped canned
        pimiento
    1 tablespoon lemon juice
    1 teaspoon finely chopped onion
    Paprika
    Crackers or tortilla chips

Combine first 5 ingredients and ¼ teaspoon salt. Place in serving bowl; sprinkle with paprika. Serve with crackers or tortilla chips. Makes about 1¼ cups.

Ham-Cheese Logs

    4 ounces sharp natural Cheddar cheese,
        shredded (1 cup)
    1 8-ounce package cream cheese
    1 4½-ounce can deviled ham
    ½ cup chopped pitted ripe olives
    ½ cup finely chopped pecans
    Crackers

Have Cheddar and cream cheeses at room temperature. In small mixer bowl beat together cheeses till blended. Beat in deviled ham; stir in chopped olives. Chill. Shape into two 8-inch long logs. Roll in pecans. Serve with crackers. Makes 2 logs.

Caviar Log

As shown at the beginning of this section —

    1 4¾-ounce can liver pâté
    1 2-ounce jar black caviar
    4 3-ounce packages cream cheese
    Melba toast rounds

Have pâté, caviar, and cheese at room temperature. Place cream cheese on waxed paper. Use the paper to roll and shape cheese into a log. Spread evenly with liver pâté, then carefully cover with caviar. Lightly cover with clear plastic wrap; chill at least 1 hour. Serve with melba toast. Makes 1 log.

Mock Quiche Squares

As shown at the beginning of this section—

5 slices white bread
5 slices bacon
2 hard-cooked eggs, thinly sliced
¼ cup sliced green onion
5 slices process Swiss cheese
    Paprika

Trim crusts from bread; toast. Cook bacon till crisp; reserve drippings and crumble bacon. Brush toast with drippings. Cut each slice of toast into quarters; sprinkle with bacon. Top *each* with egg slice; sprinkle with onion. Cut cheese slices into small squares and place one on *each* appetizer. Broil 3 inches from heat till cheese melts, about 1 to 2 minutes. Sprinkle appetizers with paprika. Makes 20.

Smoked Salmon Rolls

1 3-ounce package cream cheese, softened
2 teaspoons milk
½ teaspoon grated onion
⅛ teaspoon dried dillweed
¼ pound smoked salmon
    Cocktail crackers

Blend first 4 ingredients and ⅛ teaspoon salt. Spread evenly over salmon. Cut into strips about 3x½ inches. Roll each jelly-roll style. Chill thoroughly. Place salmon rolls on cocktail crackers. Makes 18 to 24.

Liverwurst Rolls

1 package refrigerated crescent rolls
2 4¾-ounce cans liverwurst spread
5 slices bacon, crisp-cooked, drained, and crumbled
¼ cup thinly sliced green onion

Separate roll dough at perforations. Spread with liverwurst; cut each triangle into 4 triangles. Sprinkle with bacon and onion and pat in lightly; roll up. Place on baking sheet; bake at 375° for 10 minutes. Makes 32.

Hot Beef Spread

1 8-ounce package cream cheese, softened
2 tablespoons milk
• • •
1 2½-ounce jar sliced dried beef, finely snipped (about ¾ cup)
2 tablespoons instant minced onion
2 tablespoons finely chopped green pepper
⅛ teaspoon pepper
½ cup dairy sour cream
¼ cup coarsely chopped walnuts
    Assorted crackers

Blend softened cream cheese and milk. Stir in dried beef, instant minced onion, green pepper, and pepper; mix well. Stir in dairy sour cream. Spoon into 8-inch pie plate or small shallow baking dish. Sprinkle chopped walnuts over top. Bake at 350° for 15 minutes. Serve hot with assorted crackers.

Tiny Ham Puffs

2 cups ground fully cooked ham (½ pound)
⅓ cup finely chopped celery
⅓ cup finely chopped chutney
2 tablespoons mayonnaise or salad dressing
    Dash pepper
⅔ cup water
1 stick piecrust mix, crumbled
2 eggs

In mixing bowl combine ham, celery, chutney, mayonnaise, and pepper; mix well. Chill.

In small saucepan heat water to boiling. Add crumbled piecrust mix; stir vigorously over low heat till pastry forms a ball and leaves sides of pan. Cook 1 minute more, stirring constantly. Remove from heat. Add eggs and beat on low speed of electric mixer for 2 minutes. Drop dough by teaspoons onto ungreased baking sheet. Bake at 425° till golden brown and dry, about 20 to 25 minutes. Cool on rack away from draft. Split puffs; remove inside webbing, if desired. Just before serving, fill with chilled ham mixture. Makes 42 puffs.

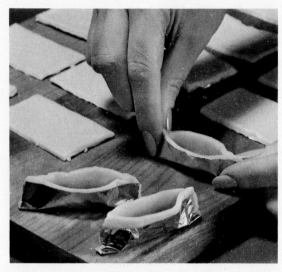

To make dainty *Salmon Boats,* roll pastry out atop foil. Cut through pastry and foil to make rectangles. Shape into boats as shown.

Shrimp Wheels

Combine one 4½-ounce can shrimp, drained and mashed; ¼ cup mayonnaise; 2 tablespoons chopped pimiento-stuffed green olives; 2 table-spoons chili sauce; and 1 tablespoon finely chopped celery. Using 1 package refrigerated crescent rolls (8 rolls), unroll dough and separate crescents into 4 rectangles. (Don't separate into triangles.) Spread *about* ¼ *cup* shrimp mixture on *each* rectangle. Starting at short end, roll up jelly-roll fashion. Cut each roll into 10 slices. Place, cut side down, on greased baking sheet. Bake at 375° for 10 to 12 minutes. Serve hot. Makes 40.

Notches

Cut 2 ounces natural Cheddar cheese into 24 pieces, each piece measuring ¾x¾x⅛ inch. Dice 1 mild chili pepper. Arrange 24 taco-flavored tortilla chips on baking sheet. Place *1 teaspoon* refried beans or canned bean dip in center of *each* chip. Top beans with pieces of cheese and chili pepper. Broil 4 inches from heat till cheese begins to melt, 1 to 3 minutes. Makes 24.

Salmon Boats

> 2 sticks piecrust mix
> 1 7¾-ounce can salmon, drained,
>   boned, and flaked
> ⅓ cup mayonnaise or salad dressing
> 1 tablespoon drained capers
> 2 teaspoons prepared mustard
>   Pimiento, cut in strips

Prepare piecrust mix according to package directions; divide in half. On a large sheet of foil, roll each half of the pastry to a 12½x9-inch rectangle. With kitchen shears, cut pastry *and* foil into 2½x1½-inch rectangles. Fold rectangles in half lengthwise. Pinch ends together to seal. Place upright on ungreased baking sheet, pressing down and in slightly to form "boat." Prick bottom of dough with fork. Bake at 450° till golden, 7 to 8 minutes. Carefully remove foil. Blend together salmon, mayonnaise or salad dressing, capers, and mustard. Fill each baked boat with about 1 teaspoon salmon mixture. Garnish with pimiento strips. Makes 60.

Stuffed Mushrooms

> 2 ounces process Swiss cheese,
>   shredded (½ cup)
> 1 hard-cooked egg, finely chopped
> 3 tablespoons fine dry bread crumbs
> ½ clove garlic, minced
> 2 tablespoons butter or margarine,
>   softened
>   • • •
> 1 pound fresh mushrooms, each about
>   1 to 1½ inches in diameter
> ¼ cup butter or margarine, melted

In mixing bowl combine shredded Swiss cheese, chopped egg, crumbs, garlic, and the 2 tablespoons softened butter; blend thoroughly. Remove stems from mushrooms; place unfilled mushrooms, rounded side up, on baking sheet. Brush tops with ¼ cup melted butter. Broil 3 to 4 inches from heat till lightly browned, 2 to 3 minutes. Remove from broiler. Turn mushrooms; fill each with cheese mixture. Return filled mushrooms to broiler; broil 1 to 2 minutes more. Makes about 36.

Cornucopias: Trim crust from bread slices. Spread each trimmed slice with softened pineapple cheese spread. Carefully roll each slice into a cornucopia as shown. Trim cornucopias with petals made from ripe olives. Place on flat pan or board, seam side down, and chill till serving time.

Fold-Ups: Trim crust from bread slices; spread with softened cheese spread. Bring two opposite corners of bread slice together at center. Secure with wooden pick and add a watercress sprig for garnish.

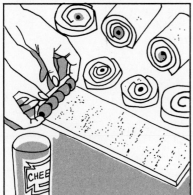

Pinwheels: Have bakery trim crusts from 1 loaf unsliced sandwich bread and cut loaf *lengthwise* in slices ¼ inch thick. (Or, at home, use an electric knife for ease in slicing bread.) Spread each slice with softened cheese spread, a meat or seafood salad mixture (ham, chicken, tuna), or parsley butter (combine butter or margarine and snipped parsley). For pretty centers, line up a row of pimiento-stuffed green olives, crosswise, near end of each slice as shown. Starting at short end, roll up jelly-roll fashion; wrap in foil or clear plastic wrap. Chill, seam side down. Before serving, place roll, seam side down, on cutting board; using sharp knife, carefully cut roll into ⅜-inch slices.

Jigsaws: Using half white and half whole wheat bread, cut bread slices into two-inch rounds. For sandwich bottoms, spread *half* the rounds of each color with seafood or cheese spread. Make tops by cutting circles from remaining bread rounds with hole of doughnut cutter. Fit tiny whole wheat circles into white rings and vice versa. Assemble sandwiches by placing tops and bottoms together. *Or,* cut bread rounds into strips or quarters; arrange atop spread, alternating colors. Another time, use tiny sandwich or cookie cutters for a variety of different bread shapes.

Checkerboards: Have bakery trim the crusts from two unsliced sandwich loaves—one white bread and one whole wheat or rye bread. From *each* loaf, cut six *lengthwise* slices about ½ inch thick. Use your favorite filling or spread to put four slices bread together, alternating white and whole wheat. Repeat to make a total of three loaves; wrap in foil, clear plastic wrap, or waxed paper; chill. Slice each loaf into six *lengthwise* slices as shown. Put four of these slices together with additional filling, alternating colors to make checkerboard loaf (see picture). Repeat to make a total of four loaves. (There will be two slices remaining; cut each of these into 4 or 5 ribbon sandwiches.) Wrap loaves and chill once more; cut each loaf *crosswise* in about ½-inch slices to make checkerboard sandwiches.

BEVERAGES

1-2-3 Easy Party Punch

Double the recipe to make 20 servings —

>   1 6-ounce can frozen orange juice
>   concentrate, thawed
>   ⅓ cup light corn syrup
>   1 28-ounce bottle ginger ale, chilled
>   Ice

Combine concentrate and syrup. Add ginger ale. Pour over ice in small punch bowl. Garnish with orange slices and strawberries, if desired. Makes 10 (4-ounce) servings.

Ruby Fruit Punch

>   1 28-ounce bottle ginger ale, chilled
>   1 tablespoon lemon juice
>   Orange slices
>   1 32-ounce bottle cranberry juice
>   cocktail, chilled* (4 cups)
>   1 cup apple juice, chilled*

Combine ginger ale, lemon juice, and a few orange slices in punch bowl. Add cranberry juice cocktail and apple juice; stir to blend. Makes 16 (4-ounce) servings.

*If desired, substitute cranberry-apple drink for the cranberry and apple juice.

Amber Tea Delight

>   4 cups hot tea
>   2 12-ounce cans apricot nectar
>   2 cups orange juice
>   ½ cup sugar
>   ½ cup lemon juice
>   1 28-ounce bottle ginger ale, chilled
>   Ice cubes

Combine hot tea, apricot nectar, orange juice, sugar, and lemon juice. Chill. Before serving, add ginger ale. Pour over ice cubes to serve. Makes about 24 (4-ounce) servings.

Strawberry Sparkle Punch

Ginger ale adds sparkle —

>   2 cups fresh strawberries, hulled
>   1 3-ounce package strawberry-
>   flavored gelatin
>   1 cup boiling water
>   1 6-ounce can frozen lemonade
>   concentrate
>
>   • • •
>
>   1 32-ounce bottle cranberry juice
>   cocktail, chilled (4 cups)
>   3 cups cold water
>   Ice
>   1 28-ounce bottle ginger ale, chilled

Put strawberries in blender container; cover and blend at low speed till fruit is pureed. Dissolve strawberry-flavored gelatin in boiling water. Stir in lemonade concentrate till melted. Add cranberry juice cocktail, cold water, and strawberry purée. Pour over ice in large punch bowl. Slowly pour in ginger ale. Makes about 30 (4-ounce) servings.

Spiced Grape Punch

Serve this hot punch when it's cold outside —

>   6 cups water
>   4 cups grape juice
>   1 cup sugar
>   1 6-ounce can frozen lemonade
>   concentrate
>   1 6-ounce can frozen orange juice
>   concentrate
>   4 inches stick cinnamon, broken
>   6 whole cloves

In large saucepan combine water, grape juice, sugar, and concentrates. Tie cinnamon and cloves in cheesecloth bag or place in tea ball; add to punch. Simmer about 15 minutes; remove spices before serving. Serve hot. Makes about 20 (4-ounce) servings.

Rosy Champagne Punch

Dark sweet cherries add color and flavor —

   2 16-ounce cans pitted dark sweet
      cherries
   1 12-ounce can pineapple juice
   ½ cup brandy
   ¼ cup lemon juice
   2 ⁴/₅-quart bottles champagne, chilled

Drain cherries, reserving 2 tablespoons syrup. Combine drained cherries, pineapple juice, brandy, lemon juice, and reserved cherry syrup. Chill thoroughly to blend flavors. Just before serving, pour into punch bowl; carefully add champagne, pouring down side of bowl. Makes 20 (4-ounce) servings.

Hot Apple Wine

   3 cups apple cider
   ¼ cup sugar
   3 inches stick cinnamon
   6 whole cloves
     Peel of ¼ lemon, cut in strips
       • • •
   1 ⁴/₅-quart bottle dry white wine
   2 tablespoons lemon juice

In saucepan combine apple cider, sugar, cinnamon, cloves, and lemon peel. Bring to boiling, stirring till sugar dissolves. Simmer, uncovered, for 15 minutes; strain to remove spices and peel. Add wine and lemon juice. Heat through, but do not boil. Serve in preheated mugs. Makes 6 to 8 servings.

Fill a punch bowl with *Rosy Champagne Punch,* pour mugs of *Hot Apple Wine,* or serve glasses of *Sherried Chocolate Frappé* topped with vanilla ice cream (see page 106).

Sherried Chocolate Frappé

2 cups milk
⅓ cup chocolate syrup
⅓ cup cream sherry
1 pint vanilla ice cream
Ground cinnamon

Combine milk, chocolate syrup, and sherry. Spoon ice cream into 4 tall glasses; pour chocolate mixture over. Muddle mixture slightly; sprinkle with cinnamon. Makes 4 servings.

Raspberry Punch

As shown at the beginning of this section—

1 10-ounce package frozen raspberries, thawed
1 6-ounce can frozen limeade concentrate, thawed
¼ cup sugar
1 28-ounce bottle lemon-lime carbonated beverage, chilled
Ice cubes

Sieve berries; discard seeds. Mix berries, limeade concentrate, 2 cups water, and sugar. Chill. At serving time, add carbonated beverage and ice. Makes 15 (4-ounce) servings.

Daiquiri Punch

2 6-ounce cans frozen limeade concentrate, thawed
1 6-ounce can frozen lemonade concentrate, thawed
1 6-ounce can frozen orange juice concentrate, thawed
1 ⅘-quart bottle rum
4 cups carbonated water, chilled
Ice Ring

Combine concentrates with 8 cups water. Chill. To serve, combine with rum in punch bowl. Carefully pour in carbonated water. Float Ice Ring in punch. Makes 30 (5-ounce) servings.

Ice Ring: Alternate canned pineapple slices, halved, and green maraschino cherries in bottom of ring mold. Fill with water; freeze.

Pitcher Champagne Punch

1 6-ounce can frozen lemonade concentrate, thawed
• • •
½ cup orange-flavored liqueur
1 ⅘-quart bottle champagne, chilled

Mix *half* the concentrate and 1½ cups water; freeze into ice cubes. At serving time, combine liqueur, remaining concentrate, and 1 cup water in 2-quart pitcher. Add lemonade cubes. Slowly pour in champagne; stir gently. Makes about 8 (5-ounce) servings.

Peach Spike

As shown at the beginning of this section—

1 10-ounce package frozen peach slices, partially thawed
1 6-ounce can frozen lemonade concentrate, partially thawed
1 lemonade can vodka or rum (⅔ cup)
12 ice cubes

In blender container combine peaches, concentrate, and vodka or rum. Blend till peaches are chopped. Add ice cubes, one at a time, blending at lowest speed till slushy. Garnish with maraschino cherries and lemon wedges, if desired. Makes 6 to 8 servings.

Hawaiian Rum Drink

1 6-ounce can frozen pineapple juice concentrate, thawed
1 cup rum
½ cup light corn syrup
¼ cup lemon juice
1 quart ice cubes

In blender container combine *half each* of the concentrate, rum, corn syrup, and lemon juice. Add *half* the ice, one cube at a time, blending at low speed till slushy. Pour into small serving glasses. Repeat with remaining half of ingredients. Garnish with fresh mint leaves, if desired. Serve immediately with short straws. Makes 8 to 10 servings.

Spiced Mocha

In small mixer bowl combine ½ cup whipping cream, 1 tablespoon sugar, 1 teaspoon instant coffee powder, ¼ teaspoon ground cinnamon, and dash ground nutmeg; whip till stiff peaks form. Put 1 tablespoon chocolate syrup in *each* of 6 coffee cups. Fill cups with hot coffee; stir gently. Top with dollops of the spiced whipped cream. Serves 6.

Hot Malted-Mint Drink

As shown at the beginning of this section —

6 chocolate-covered cream-filled
   mint patties
5 cups milk
½ cup chocolate malted milk powder
1 teaspoon vanilla
   Whipped cream

In saucepan combine mint patties and *1 cup* milk. Heat and stir over low heat till mint patties are melted. Stir in remaining milk, malted milk powder, and vanilla. Heat slowly just till boiling. Beat with rotary beater till frothy. Pour into cups and top with dollops of whipped cream. Makes 6 servings.

Lime-Frosted Punch

2 cups sugar
3 envelopes unsweetened lemon-lime
   flavored soft drink powder
3 cups pineapple-grapefruit drink,
   chilled
⅓ cup lemon juice
1 quart lime sherbet
1 32-ounce bottle lemon-lime
   carbonated beverage, chilled

In punch bowl combine sugar and soft drink powder. Add next 2 ingredients and 6 cups cold water; stir till sugar dissolves. Stir *half* of the sherbet to soften; blend into punch mixture. Top with scoops of remaining sherbet. Resting bottle on rim of bowl, carefully pour in carbonated beverage; stir gently. Makes 36 (4-ounce) servings.

Eggnog

Delicious with or without the liquor —

12 eggs
½ cup sugar
 4 cups cold milk
¼ teaspoon salt
½ cup bourbon*
½ to ¾ cup light rum*
      • • •
2 cups whipping cream
   Ground nutmeg

Separate eggs. In small mixer bowl beat egg yolks. Gradually add sugar and beat till thick and lemon-colored. Add milk, salt, bourbon, and rum. Whip cream. In very large bowl beat egg whites till stiff but not dry. Fold egg yolk mixture and whipped cream into egg whites. Serve immediately in chilled punch bowl. Sprinkle ground nutmeg over each serving. Makes about 25 (5-ounce) servings.

*If desired, substitute cold milk for the bourbon and light rum.

Quantity Egg Coffee

2 slightly beaten eggs (reserve
   shells)
2¼ to 2½ cups regular-grind coffee
10 quarts cold water

In a large kettle combine eggs, crumbled egg shells, and coffee. Pour in water. Bring to boiling. Stir when foam starts to appear and continue stirring until foam disappears.

Remove from heat; let settle. If necessary, add 1 cup cold water to aid settling. Strain with fine mesh strainer or cloth before serving. Makes 50 (¾ cup) servings.

Quantity Tea

Tie 1 cup tea leaves loosely in cheesecloth bag. Place tea leaves or 40 individual tea bags in large kettle. Bring 9 quarts cold water to a boil; immediately pour over tea. Cover; steep tea 3 to 5 minutes. Remove tea and serve. Makes 50 (about ¾-cup) servings.

Martini

Traditional: Combine 1 jigger dry gin or vodka (1½ ounces), 1 tablespoon dry vermouth (½ ounce), and cracked ice. Stir and strain into a chilled cocktail glass. Add a lemon twist or an olive. For a **Gibson,** add a pearl onion instead of the olive. Makes 1.

Dry: Use 5 parts dry gin or vodka and 1 part dry vermouth.

Extra Dry: Use 7 parts dry gin or vodka (if only extra dry, not extra strong, use 80-proof) and 1 part dry vermouth.

Manhattan

Traditional: Combine 1 jigger blended whiskey or bourbon (1½ ounces), 1 tablespoon sweet vermouth (½ ounce), a dash of bitters, and cracked ice. Stir and strain into a chilled cocktail glass. Garnish with a maraschino cherry. Makes 1.

Dry: Substitute dry vermouth for sweet vermouth and serve with an olive.

Perfect: Combine 1 jigger bourbon, ½ jigger dry vermouth, ½ jigger sweet vermouth, and cracked ice. Stir and strain into chilled glass.

Daiquiri

    1 jigger light rum (1½ ounces)
    ½ jigger lime juice (¾ ounce)
      Confectioners' sugar
    1 teaspoon Triple Sec (optional)
      Crushed ice

Blend in blender or shake in cocktail shaker rum, juice, confectioners' sugar to taste, Triple Sec, and ice. Strain into stemmed cocktail glass. Makes 1.

Bloody Mary

Shake in a cocktail shaker 2 jiggers tomato juice (3 ounces), 1 jigger vodka or gin (1½ ounces), juice of ½ lemon, dash Worcestershire sauce, celery salt to taste, pepper to taste, and chopped ice. Strain into a 6-ounce cocktail glass. Garnish with lemon slice. Makes 1.

Whiskey Sour

Shake in cocktail shaker 2 jiggers bourbon, Scotch, or rye (3 ounces); ½ jigger lemon or lime juice (¾ ounce); 1 teaspoon confectioners' sugar; and 3 or 4 ice cubes. Strain into glass. Garnish with lemon slice and maraschino cherry. Makes 1.

Collins

Combine in a cocktail shaker 1 jigger vodka or gin (1½ ounces), 1½ teaspoons superfine sugar, and juice of ½ lemon. Shake well. Pour into an ice-filled highball glass and add club soda to fill. Makes 1.

Highball

In a highball glass combine 2 or 3 ice cubes and 2 ounces Scotch, rye, or bourbon. Fill glass with water, club soda, or ginger ale. Stir to mix. Makes 1.

Grasshopper

    1 jigger white crème de cacao
    1 jigger green crème de menthe
    1 tablespoon heavy cream
    3 or 4 ice cubes

Shake all ingredients in cocktail shaker. Strain into a cocktail glass. Makes 1.

Screwdriver

Place 2 or 3 ice cubes and 2 jiggers vodka (3 ounces) in highball glass. Fill with orange juice; stir. Garnish with an orange slice or a maraschino cherry. Makes 1.

Tonic

Combine juice and rind of ¼ lime; 1 jigger gin, vodka, or tequila (1½ ounces); and ice cubes in a tall glass. Fill with tonic water. Stir to mix. Makes 1.

BASIC BAR

Stocking a bar can pose problems if you don't know what and how much to buy. To avoid the expense and the embarrassment of mistakes, follow these guidelines:

Good drinks are made of good ingredients, so buy the best liquor and mixes you can afford. Buy unfamiliar liquors in small quantities until you're sure of your preferences, then buy larger, more economical sizes. Use the following list to decide what you need.

Liquor for minimum bar
  Scotch and/or bourbon and/or blended rye whiskey
  Gin
  Dry and/or sweet vermouth (keep dry vermouth refrigerated after opening)
  Before-dinner drink (aperitif)—dry or medium sherry
  After-dinner drink—brandy and/or liqueur
  Beer (if cold, keep refrigerated)
Liquor for a full-capacity bar
  Include all the liquor given above for minimum bar plus vodka, rum, tequila, and a selection of liqueurs and brandy.
Bar tools
  Both a corkscrew and a bottle opener
  A good paring knife
  Juicer with coarse strainer
  Ice crusher and ice cube cracker
  Bar spoon; bar strainer
  Two-sided measure—jigger (1½ ounces) on one side and pony (1 ounce) on the other
  Ice bucket and tongs
  Plenty of coasters or jackets
  Long and short straws
  Drink mixer-shaker; blender
  Glassware—assorted types
Other needs
  Mixers including club soda, ginger ale, cola drinks, tonic water, other carbonated beverages, and tomato juice
  Citrus fruit for juice, peel, and slices
  Syrups and liqueurs as needed
  Angostura and other bitters as needed
  Sugar and/or simple syrup (equal parts of sugar and water boiled for 5 minutes)
  Pitted green olives, cocktail onions, and maraschino cherries with stems
  Pitcher of water and bucket of ice

COCKTAIL PARTIES
(see index for page numbers of recipes)

SMALL-SIZED GROUPS

A selection of alcoholic and nonalcoholic beverages plus
Yogurt-Cuke Dip
Stuffed Eggs
Notches or Smoked Salmon Rolls
or
Creamy Blue Cheese Dip
Avocado-Beef Spread
Mock Quiche Squares

MEDIUM-SIZED GROUPS

A selection of alcoholic and nonalcoholic beverages plus
Dill-Sour Cream Dip
Hot Beef Spread
Nibble Mix (half recipe)
Shrimp Wheels or Liverwurst Rolls
or
Hot Cheese-Chive Dip
Stuffed Mushrooms
Pinwheels (half recipe)

LARGE-SIZED GROUPS

A selection of alcoholic and nonalcoholic beverages plus
Prairie Fire
Nibble Mix
Pinwheels or Cornucopias
or
Creamy Blue Cheese Dip (double recipe)
Hot Cheese-Chive Dip (double recipe)
Nibble Mix
Tiny Ham Puffs

WINES AND AFTER-DINNER DRINKS

Are you confused when it comes to choosing the right type of wine to serve with certain foods? You needn't be because there are no definite rules that must be followed. However, some guidelines have been established to help you enjoy wine to the fullest.

Wines can be divided into four general classes: appetizer or aperitif wines, dinner wines, dessert wines, and sparkling wines. The name of the class generally indicates the use of each. Appetizer wines, for example, stimulate the appetite and are usually dry. (In reference to wines, dry means "not sweet.")

The dinner wines, also called table wines, include both red and white wines. They are usually served with the main course. Red dinner wines are predominately dry and rich and sometimes have a tart or astringent characteristic, so they are best with hearty or highly seasoned foods. White dinner wines, on the other hand, are lighter in flavor and can be very dry and tart or sweet. Serve white wines with delicately flavored foods so that the flavor of the wine doesn't overpower the entrée. Rosé wine is an all-purpose dinner wine, compatible with any type of food.

Dessert wines are sweeter wines, and, as the name implies, they are served at the last course of the meal or in place of dessert.

Like Rosé, sparkling wines complement any food, or they can be served by themselves. Sparkling wines are all-purpose and can be served before, during, or at the end of the meal. Familiar sparkling wines include Champagne, Sparkling Burgundy, and Cold Duck.

When deciding how much wine to buy, allow 4 to 6 glasses from a fifth (25.6 fluid ounces) of dinner and sparkling wines, and 10 to 12 glasses from a fifth of appetizer and dessert wines. Each glass of wine is based on 4 to 6 ounces of dinner or sparkling wine and 2 to 2½ ounces of appetizer or dessert wine. Be sure to plan for refills.

Store unopened wines away from the sun at a cool, constant temperature (about 60°). Place a corked bottle on its side so that the cork will stay moist. A bottle with a screw cap can be placed upright or on its side.

Knowing the correct serving temperature for the various wines is also helpful. The majority of the Rosé and white wines are served prechilled to a temperature of 45° to 50°. Sparkling wines are served at a temperature of 40° to 45°. Appetizer, dessert, and red dinner wines are generally served at a cool room temperature (60° to 70°), except for dry Sherry and dry Vermouth, which are chilled to 45° to 55° or served over ice.

There are a few additional pointers you should know about serving wine. Open red dinner wines about 1 hour before serving to allow the wine to "breathe" and to develop its bouquet. However, wait until just before serving to open other wines.

When serving wine, use clear, stemmed glasses that are completely dry and free of lint, film, and waterspots. Pour a small amount of wine in your glass first and sample it. (This is done to remove any stray pieces of cork and to detect a vinegary flavored wine.) Then, fill each guest's glass ⅓ to ½ full for a still wine. For sparkling wines, pour wine into the glass until the foam reaches the rim; continue filling the glass until it is ⅔ to ¾ full.

After-dinner drinks include both brandy and liqueurs. Cognac, a top-quality grape brandy from France, and other fine brandies are usually served straight in snifters. Brandy is also served in coffee or over ice. In addition, there are other fruit-flavored brandies. These are usually identified by the fruit name, such as apple brandy or pear brandy. However, some fruit brandies have their own names, such as Kirsch (cherry); Framboise (raspberry); Calvados (apple); Quetsch, Slivovitz, and Mirabelle (plum); and Williamine (pear).

Liqueurs, also called cordials, are sweet and have various flavors. Examples of familiar liqueurs include Grand Marnier and Cointreau (orange), Kahlua (coffee), Crème de Cacao (chocolate), and Crème de Menthe (peppermint). Benedictine and Chartreuse are liqueurs prepared with special herb formulas.

Serve liqueurs in small glasses, straight or over ice in larger glasses. Or, if you wish, pour liqueurs over ice cream.

Appetizer wines, also referred to as aperitifs, are those served before a meal or as a cocktail. Dry wines are usually preferred over the sweeter types. Appetizer wines include dry Sherry, Vermouth, and flavored wines. Serve them in an all-purpose wineglass, or choose the 6-ounce glass. These wines are best with all types of appetizers.

White dinner (table) wines are delicately flavored and are generally served with light foods such as poultry, fish, shellfish, and veal. Examples of white wines include Chablis, white Burgundy, Rhine, dry Sauterne, and white Chianti. The flavor varies from very dry and tart to sweet and full-bodied. Use the 8- to 10-ounce all-purpose wineglass.

Red dinner (table) wines are generally robust in flavor, thus, they complement hearty foods such as red meats (beef and pork), cheese, egg, and pasta dishes, and highly seasoned foods. Red dinner wines include red Burgundy, Claret (Bordeaux), red Chianti, and Rosé. Serve red dinner wines in the 8- to 10-ounce all-purpose wineglass.

Dessert wines have a special sweetness and richness. Because of these characteristics, they are served as the dessert or as a dessert accompaniment. Dessert wines go especially well with fruits, nuts, and dessert cheeses. Examples include Port, Tokay, Muscatel, sweet Sauterne, and sweet or cream Sherry. Serve dessert wines in 4-ounce glasses.

Party Hints

Whether you're new to the world of entertaining or a more experienced homemaker who is searching for additional ideas and help with entertaining, you'll find information here that will make party planning enjoyable. You will find tips on how to be the relaxed and organized hostess— from planning the party to seeing your guests to the door at the end of the party, plus a few tips on how to manage unexpected company.

In addition, this section provides information on table appointments and how to set the table for a sit-down meal or for buffet-style service.

You'll also find ideas for some easily created centerpieces that will make your table look impressive and give it that individual touch.

Flowers of all types make colorful centerpieces, whether it's a fresh bouquet of brilliant Ranunculus, a handful of cardinal red geraniums, or flowers handmade with plastic pellets or straw daisies made on a loom.

BEING A GOOD HOSTESS

A relaxed, confident hostess is the key to a successful party. If you show signs of uneasiness or act unsure of yourself, the guests will sense your discomfort and may not have a good time. The best way to avoid entertaining catastrophes is to plan well.

If you are a really good hostess, you'll plan everything well in advance, from deciding how many guests to invite to what style of food service will be used. Then, when guests arrive, you and the host will be in complete control of the situation. If your entertaining attempts thus far leave much to be desired, read through this section before planning your next party. It will be time well spent.

PLANNING

The very first thing you should do when planning your party is to decide how many guests to invite. This is a relatively simple matter, but don't forget to consider four things—how many you can comfortably handle, the capacity of your home, the type and amount of equipment you have, and your budget.

The organized hostess

How many you can comfortably handle is the biggest factor as far as the number of guests is concerned. If you're entertaining a very large group, it is best to get some help. Things will go much smoother that way.

The capacity of your home also has a direct bearing on the number of persons you can invite. If you are planning a sit-down meal, the size of the dining table is also important. One thing that many people fail to realize is that entertaining is not limited to the living and dining rooms. You can also use the family room, patio, porch, or the basement.

The type and amount of equipment you have may also influence the number of guests, and as such, is worth considering. However, if you want to have a large party even though you lack certain necessities, you can always rent tables, chairs, dinnerware, glassware, cooking containers, heating equipment, and other items.

Churches and local women's clubs are also good sources of entertaining equipment, especially if you're looking for a large coffee maker or tables and chairs. If you serve large numbers of people only once or twice a year, it is usually easier and less costly to rent or borrow what you need than it is to buy and store items that you seldom use.

Your budget, that ever-present guardian against overspending, also may be a deciding factor in the number of people you can invite to your party, or in the type of party you give. For example, a brunch for eight often is less expensive than a dinner for six or a cocktail party for twelve because of the costs of the foods and beverages served.

Here are some hints that may help you to cut the cost of party giving. Have parties on successive days or try two kinds of parties on the same day, such as a brunch in mid-morning and a cocktail party in the evening. By doing this, you can use the same flowers, perhaps cook some of the foods in quantity, and have all of your party equipment set out, clean, and ready to use. In addition, the house will require only a little picking up and a light dusting between occasions.

Another way to cut party costs is to go easy on liquor. Punches made with wine are less expensive to serve than are cocktails, and a bottle of liquor extended with various fruit juices and mixers goes a long way. If you decide to have a bar with mixed drinks, keep control of the pouring and mixing yourself. If after-dinner drinks are on the menu, instead of offering an assortment of liqueurs, serve Irish coffee or a nonalcoholic coffee such as Espresso or Cappuccino. Always make sure that you have something special to offer guests who prefer nonalcoholic beverages.

Now that you know approximately how many people you're going to invite, decide what kind of party to have. While making your decision, keep in mind what your guests will enjoy and the type of entertaining you like to do best. Both of these things will add to the relaxed atmosphere of the party.

If your guest list is small, you probably can manage a sit-down dinner. For a medium-sized group, however, consider having a buffet-type meal where either you prepare all the food, or where guests bring some of it, potluck-style. An assortment of snacks and beverages is usually best for a very large group.

Regardless of the type of party you have, you will spend a considerable amount of time trying to decide what and where to serve your guests—that is, if you're like most people. This needn't be the case. Consider the following advice. If your party is to have a special theme, let this decide your menu. For example, at an oriental-themed party, consider serving a stir-fried entrée cooked at the dinner table in a wok. If you decide on an appetizer buffet, set up a buffet table in the dining room and serve snack-type foods. This way, the guests can circulate between the dining and living rooms. Should you decide on a buffet supper, set up tray tables or card tables in the living room, and set food on the buffet table in the dining room.

One of the easiest tasks in planning for a party is making up the guest list. If you invite the right combination of people—those with common interests and a mixture of occupations—everyone will enjoy themselves. It's as simple as that. If, on the other hand, you try to fulfill all of your obligations at one time, the results can be disastrous.

Remember: You should consider your guests' enjoyment, not your own social obligations, so invite people to a party that you know they'll enjoy attending.

By the way, so that you aren't disappointed by a poor turnout at your party, make sure that guests know the correct party date. Invitations can be written or telephoned for most types of informal and semiformal occasions. If you are sending invitations, whether they are hand-written or whether you fill in the information on preprinted invitations, mail them to your guests from 10 to 14 days before the party date. This allows your guests time to R.S.V.P. (please reply) to the invitation. Telephoned invitations are also permissible and should be done at least a week before the party. If possible, try to call all your guests the same day, especially if you are planning a small gathering. When telephoning invitations, be sure that you let guests know the date, time, type of party, and type of attire that is expected.

After the guests have been invited, the best thing for you to do is to put yourself on a schedule—a written schedule. From now on, timing is very important so as to avoid last-minute chaos. Writing out the menu, along with the serving dishes you intend to use,

The unorganized hostess

should be at the top of the list. Other items that you'll want to include are cleaning the house, checking the table linens, polishing the silver, planning table settings and style of service, centerpieces, candles, and other decorations, writing up the market order for both food and liquor, ordering any specialty foods, planning time for purchasing both staples and perishables, plus time for food preparation. In addition, plan what you are going to wear and be sure to allow some time on the schedule to relax and get ready before guests are expected to arrive.

Plan to do as much of the work ahead as possible. Chores such as heavy housecleaning and preparation of foods that can be frozen or refrigerated should be completed before the day of the party.

When you are planning the menu, be sure that you consider the use of make-ahead foods. Try not to plan a menu that includes more than one or two items requiring last-minute preparation.

Also, check to see that table linens are spotlessly clean and pressed well in advance of the party so that you will have ample time to launder and iron them, if necessary. In addition, make sure that you have enough napkins that are ready to use.

One duty that definitely should not be left to the day of the party is shopping for the food. If left to the last minute, shopping will take up much of your precious time, and there is always a chance that you might forget an ingredient that is needed in recipe preparation. Staple items, such as canned goods, and liquor, can be purchased well ahead of time. Then, a day before the party, you can shop for the perishable foods.

If you don't already have a party log, now is the time to start one. It can prove invaluable for future parties. Use a notebook, card file, or any other system that works for you. Include in your log any information about parties you've given that you think will be helpful in planning future parties. Things that you might include in the log are the date and time of the party, who was invited, who accepted and attended, the foods that were served and serving dishes, how the food was served, how you organized the party, equipment used, a sample table setting, decorations, and possibly the entertainment provided. You

might also include your party clothes, the likes and dislikes of guests, and any other helpful information.

When the day of the party arrives, make any final food preparations and do a bit of touch-up cleaning. Just before the party, check to see that the guest bathroom is spotless and that fresh soap and towels are handy. You might also arrange a beauty tray for female guests. On it place a new comb, a can of hair spray, and a box of facial tissues.

Also, before guests arrive, be sure that you have plenty of ashtrays and coasters placed around the party room. Ashtrays should be emptied at regular intervals, so have a suitable container for this purpose.

PARTY TIME

You're relaxed, confident, and ready (thanks to careful planning). Now, handle each situation as it comes and follow through with plans.

If possible, both host and hostess should greet guests at the door and make them feel welcome. Although this may become difficult as more guests arrive, make sure that someone is always near the door to greet latecomers.

What to do with guests' coats may pose a problem, so clear out the hall closet ahead of time and have plenty of hangers available. For large parties, hang the men's coats in the closet and let the women place their coats in one of the bedrooms. This will give the ladies a chance to freshen up a bit before joining the party.

If yours is a small party, introduce the newly arrived guests to everyone. However, for a larger party, only introduce the new arrivals to a few people, then let them introduce themselves to others. The host and hostess should visit with each guest during the party.

There are several other points to keep in mind during the party, too. It's a good idea to try to avoid having both the host and hostess out of the room at one time. Also, be aware of your guests' comfort during the party. If the room temperature gets too warm, open a window or door, or turn down the thermostat. Should you or your guests become bothered by cigarette, cigar, or pipe smoke, light some candles to help clear the air.

If you are hosting a sit-down dinner party, be sure that guests are not crowded together at the table. At a sit-down meal for more than six, it's best to have place cards to avoid the scramble for chairs. Use plain white cards on which names are clearly written. For parties with less than six people, have the seating arrangement in mind before you announce that dinner is ready to be served.

Traditionally, the hostess is seated at one end of the table (closest to the kitchen) and the host is seated at the opposite end. Seat a male guest of honor to the right of the hostess or an honored female guest to the right of the host. The dinner partner of the guest of honor should sit at the opposite end to the right of either host or hostess, depending on whom the guest of honor is. The second most important male guest should be seated to the hostess' left and the second most important female guest should be seated to the host's left. Alternate men and women around the table, if possible.

When you're serving snacks rather than a sit-down meal, place the food in an easily accessible area and have plenty of napkins on hand. For this informal type of gathering, consider using coaster trays, as they will hold both drinks and snacks easily.

At the end of the party when guests are leaving, the host should get the coats from the closet and the hostess should accompany women guests to the bedroom where they have placed their coats. The host and/or hostess should then see the guests to the door and remain at the open door until the guests are safely on their way.

STYLES OF FOOD SERVICE

One of the items on your schedule that needs to be thought out well in advance of the party is how you are going to serve the food. There are several service styles that can be used. These styles include continental service, English service, family-style, country-style, blue-plate service, and buffet-style.

Continental service, also referred to as formal or Russian service, requires servants, so it is rarely used. When it is used, the food is arranged on the plate, then the filled plate is placed before guests; or empty plates are placed before guests who help themselves to food passed by servants; or empty plates are placed before guests and the food is served onto the plates by servants.

English service is another service style. The dinner plates are stacked in front of the host, who serves the meat. He, in turn, passes the plates to the hostess, who serves the vegetables. Then, the plates are passed to guests. A variation of this style is *family-style service,* sometimes called compromise service. For this style, all the food for the entrée is served by one person, then the filled plates are passed to guests in an orderly manner.

Other popular service styles include *country-style service* and *blue-plate service.* For country-style service, filled serving dishes are placed on the table and the guest closest to the dish helps himself and passes the dish to the person on his right. Blue-plate service entails filling the plates in the kitchen, then placing the filled plate on the table just before guests sit down at the dinner table.

Buffet-style is another type of service. Containers of food are placed on a suitable surface, such as a side buffet, table, or counter. Electric warming trays or electric skillets are ideal for keeping foods hot on the buffet table. Guests help themselves to the food, then they sit down at set tables, balance plates or trays on their laps, or set plates on small tray tables placed around the room.

UNEXPECTED COMPANY

There always seem to be occasions when you don't have time to prepare for guests, such as when friends stop by. To avoid embarrassment on the part of your surprise visitors, be prepared for such occasions by having an emergency supply of food. Foods that are handy to have on hand include casseroles that have been frozen or the ingredients for dishes that can be quickly combined. Taping a quick-to-prepare recipe to a paper bag filled with shelf-stable ingredients for the recipe is also a good idea. This eliminates hunting for a recipe and ingredients when time is short. Taking precautions like these will make your unexpected company feel welcome.

SPECIAL HELPS

TABLE APPOINTMENTS

A dinner table that looks attractive makes any meal more enjoyable for your guests. This being the case, make sure that your table appointments—dinnerware, glassware, flatware, holloware, table coverings, napkins, and decorations—blend together in color, scale, and proportion. Your guests will appreciate the extra effort, and you'll know that you have done your utmost to make the meal a pleasurable occasion.

The most prominent item on any dinner table is dinnerware. There are many types of dinnerware on the market today—china, earthenware, pottery, stoneware, plastic, glass, and glass-ceramic. It's helpful to have two sets, one for everyday or for more informal entertaining, and a second set of finer china for special occasions. However, some types of dinnerware, such as a simply designed, finer type of earthenware, will do double duty and are suitable for almost any occasion.

When entertaining, most people need at least six place settings of matched dinnerware. If you entertain larger groups fairly often, however, you'll probably want to invest in additional settings. A place setting usually includes a dinner plate, dessert or salad plate, bread-and-butter plate, and a cup and saucer.

Glassware is another important table appointment. There are two styles of glassware—stemmed and unfooted—both of which come in many sizes. If you have two sets of dinnerware, you'll probably also want two sets of glassware, one for casual occasions and one for more formal occasions. For example, when using fine china, you might use stemmed crystal; however, with heavy-looking pottery, unfooted, colored glasses are a good choice.

And don't forget the flatware, the implements used for eating and serving. Sterling silver, plated silver, and stainless steel are the most popular types. Choose flatware that is appropriate with your dinnerware. For example, if you are using casual pottery, you probably would use stainless flatware.

Holloware, too, is an item to consider. These are the metal containers, such as pitchers, trays, and beverage containers, used to hold foods. They are available in the same types of materials as the flatware, plus pewter, copper, and brass.

If you already have your dinnerware, glassware, flatware, and holloware, one easy way to give your table setting an entirely different look is by purchasing new table coverings. And what a selection there is. Tablecloths, place mats, and table runners come in a wide range of easy-care fabrics and materials and in a variety of colors and designs.

Here are a few guidelines to help you determine which table covering to use. When using heavily patterned dinnerware, use a plain cloth. However, simply designed or plain dinnerware harmonizes with either plain or patterned cloths. If the dinnerware is heavy looking, choose a textured fabric; use more delicate-looking cloths with finer china and glassware.

Be sure that you know the size—both length and width—and the shape of your table when purchasing tablecloths. Plan to have at least a 10- to 15-inch overhang on the sides and ends of the table for an informal dinner cloth.

Place mats often are used for informal entertaining. They come in various sizes and shapes, ranging from 16 to 18 inches long and from 12 to 14 inches wide.

Table runners also can be used as a table covering, either directly on the tabletop, coordinated with place mats, or over a cloth. Runners should be about 12 inches wide and may fit the length of the table exactly or have a drop of 8 to 10 inches on both ends.

Napkins also need to be considered when planning the table setting. Oftentimes, they come in sets with the tablecloth or place mats. Dinner napkins should be made of fabric and be at least 18 inches square; for formal occasions, 24 inches square is a better size. Luncheon and breakfast napkins are 15 to 17 inches square, while cocktail napkins are 4 by 6 inches or 6 by 8 inches. Paper napkins may be used for some informal occasions.

TABLE SETTINGS

Making your dinner table a truly enjoyable place to eat involves more than just having the right combination of table appointments. You have to know how to set the table correctly, too. Here are some basic rules to follow.

Depending on the style of service you use (see page 117), the dinner plates are set in the center of each place setting, or in a stack in front of the person who will be serving. Allow about 15 inches between place settings.

When arranging forks, knives, and spoons, remember to place these items from the outside in, in the order they will be used. The china, flatware, and napkin should be placed in a line about one inch from the table edge.

Forks are placed to the left of the plate. The salad fork, if used, may be placed on either side of the dinner fork, depending on when the salad is to be served. If the salad is served before the main course, the salad fork goes to the left of the dinner fork. If the salad is eaten with or after the main course, the salad fork usually is placed to the right of the dinner fork. A salad fork is not essential if the salad accompanies the main course.

Knives and spoons are placed to the right of the plate, with the knife closest to the plate and the blade facing the plate. If the dessert requires a spoon, place two teaspoons to the right of the knife. If desired, you can bring in the dessert flatware with the dessert.

Place napkins to the left of the forks with the open corners of the napkin at the lower right. Optional placements of the napkin are on the dinner plate or in the center of the place setting between the forks and knife. These alternate napkin placements often are used when space is limited.

If a bread-and-butter plate is used, place it above the forks, with the bread-and-butter knife straight across the top of the plate. Omit this plate if space is limited.

The salad plate may take several placements. If a bread-and-butter plate is used, place the salad plate to the left and below the bread-and-butter plate. When no bread-and-butter plate is used, place the salad plate at the tip of the forks.

When placing glassware on the table, set the water glass or goblet at the tip of the knife. The wine glasses are placed above the spoons, below and to the right of the water glass.

Table set for family-style service.

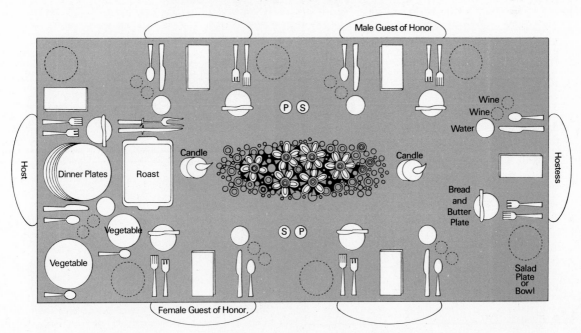

1.

2.

3.

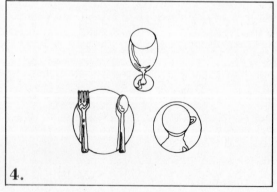

4.

Drawings at left show how to set the table. **(1)** *Appetizer course:* Provide seafood fork, if needed, napkin, and silverware and glassware for the rest of the meal. Serve the appetizer on an underliner plate. **(2)** *Soup course:* Provide a soup spoon. Place soup bowl on underliner plate. **(3)** *Main course:* Provide dinner plate, salad plate (optional), bread-and-butter plate and knife (optional), dinner fork, salad fork (optional), knife and spoon. Provide a glass for each beverage. If no previous courses have been served, include a napkin. **(4)** *Dessert course:* Serve dessert from the kitchen accompanied by the silverware needed and coffee, if desired.

One-line buffet

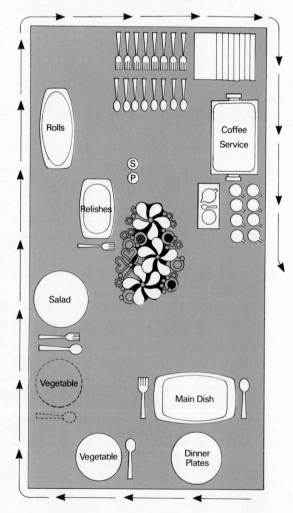

BUFFET TABLES

To make sure that everything proceeds smoothly when you are serving a buffet meal, heed the following advice.

First, plan what table you are going to put the food on and where you are going to place this table. If space permits, place the buffet table in the center of the room so that guests can walk around it. This will permit you to use either the one-line buffet, which includes beverage service, or, for large groups, the two-line buffet. If the buffet table is small or needs to be placed against a wall, use a separate table or cart for the beverage.

Next, plan the placement of food and appointments on the table. The important thing to remember is to place things in a logical sequence—dinner plates, main dish, vegetable, salad, relishes, rolls, silverware, napkins, and beverage. When setting the buffet table, be sure to allow room near each serving dish so that guests can set their plates down while they serve themselves.

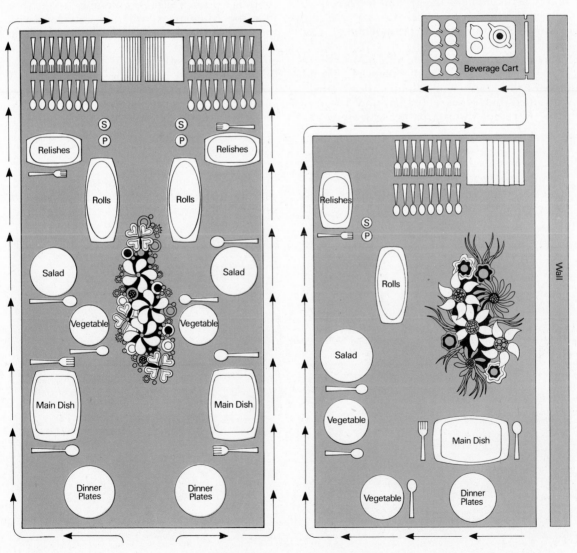

Two-line buffet

Buffet with beverage cart

CENTERPIECES

Does your table setting still lack that certain something? Then maybe a centerpiece is just what you need to add.

If thinking of an idea for a centerpiece is a problem for you, start with the traditional materials—flowers and candles. An attractive bouquet of flowers or an arrangement of candles will beautify any table. To give a new look to those old standbys, use a unique holder. For example, odds and ends of glassware make attractive vases, a large champagne glass is just right for holding a single floating flower, decorative casserole dishes hold large flower arrangements nicely, and a trivet is an attractive base for a candle. Also try building a candle into a flower arrangement. The result will be enchanting.

Actually, almost anything can be used in a centerpiece. Make use of materials found around the house. For example, use a small, unframed mirror as a background for tiny glass swans, fill a wicker basket with an assort-ment of fresh fruit, turn a large brandy snifter into a Christmas centerpiece by filling it with colorful Christmas balls, make a treasure chest from a shoe box, or use several clocks for a New Year's Eve centerpiece.

You can also take advantage of nature's materials. Turn a small tree branch into a miniature tree and fill it with Easter egg or gumdrop blossoms, gather colorful fall leaves and use them as a background for ceramic forest animals, or make a pretty fall centerpiece from dried flowers and Indian corn. Remember, these ideas are only a beginning. Now, just use your imagination.

When arranging and placing centerpieces, there are a few rules to remember. Make sure that the centerpiece will not interfere with the view of the person across the table. When candles are used, be sure that the flame is either above or below eye level. At formal dinners, always place the centerpiece of flowers and candles in the center of the table. Other times, place the centerpiece on the table wherever it looks the best.

Arrange real vegetables and vegetable candles on a scale for an unusual centerpiece. Fold the napkin decoratively for more interest.

Combine a bouquet of daisies and a glass figurine for a springy centerpiece. Unite the two centerpiece parts with a cloth background.

EQUIVALENTS

1 cup cake flour = 1 cup minus 2 tablespoons all-purpose flour

1 tablespoon cornstarch (for thickening) = 2 tablespoons all-purpose flour or 4 teaspoons quick-cooking tapioca

1 cup chocolate wafer crumbs = 19 wafers

1 cup finely crushed graham cracker crumbs = 14 square crackers

1 cup finely crushed vanilla wafer crumbs = 22 wafers

1 cup whipping cream, whipped = 2 cups whipped dessert topping

1 clove garlic = ⅛ teaspoon garlic powder

1 teaspoon dry mustard = 1 tablespoon prepared mustard

1 tablespoon fresh snipped herbs = 1 teaspoon dried herbs

1 cup uncooked macaroni = 2 cups cooked macaroni

1 cup uncooked noodles = 1 cup cooked noodles

1 cup uncooked long grain rice = 3 cups cooked rice

1 cup uncooked, packaged precooked rice = 2 cups cooked rice

7 ounces uncooked spaghetti = 4 cups cooked spaghetti

GLOSSARY

Bouquet Garni—A bundle of herbs, basically made with thyme, parsley, and bay leaf.

Café—The French word for coffee.

Canapé—An appetizer with an edible base. Canapés are usually finger foods.

Chafing Dish—A piece of cooking equipment consisting of two pans—a metal pan for the food (blazer pan) and a container for water (bain-marie)—that fit together and sit on a frame above a heat source.

Châteaubriand—A very thick, center cut taken from the beef tenderloin.

Clarified Butter—The clear, oil-like top layer poured from melted butter.

Consommé—A clear, rich soup made by boiling down meat or poultry broth until its volume is reduced by about half.

Coquille—An authentic or artificial scallop shell used for baking and attractively serving many seafood and creamed mixtures.

Crepe—A thin, delicate pancake.

Crouton—A small cube of bread that has been oven-toasted or browned in butter.

Demitasse—1. A dark, fragrant coffee usually served after dinner. 2. The small half-size cup used for serving the dark coffee.

Escargot—An edible land snail.

Fillet—1. Boned meat removed from poultry, fish, or game. 2. The process of removing meat from the bones of poultry, fish, or game.

Flambé—The French word for the flaming of food, either during preparation or when brought to the table for serving.

Hors d'oeuvre—A small, usually elegant appetizer served before a meal or at cocktail parties where no other food is served.

Liqueur—An alcoholic beverage made of a distilled spirit, a syrup, and flavorings.

Liquor—A distilled alcoholic beverage, such as whiskey, vodka, or rum.

Marinate—To allow a food to stand several hours in a seasoned liquid.

Pâté—A spreadable mixture made of meat and seasonings. The meat used for pâtés is so finely chopped or mashed that the mixture is the consistency of a paste.

Petits Fours—Small, individual cakes, biscuits, cookies, or confections. Best known are tiny pieces of cake coated with a fondantlike icing and intricately decorated.

Sauté—To cook quickly in just a little fat.

Vinaigrette—A thin, clear mixture of vinegar, oil, and seasonings that is essentially the original French salad dressing.

INDEX

A-B